From
Losers
to
Winners

From
Losers
to
Winners

*How to Manage Problem
Employees . . .
And
What to Do If You Can't*

Revised Edition

V. Clayton Sherman

American Management Association

This publication is designed to provide accurate and authoritative information in regard to the subject matter covered. It is sold with the understanding that the publisher is not engaged in rendering legal, accounting, or other professional service. If legal advice or other expert assistance is required, the services of a competent professional person should be sought.

Library of Congress Cataloging-in-Publication Data

Sherman, V. Clayton
    From losers to winners.

    Includes index.
    1. Problem employees.   I. Title.
HF5549.5.E42S54   1987b   658.3'045   87-47710
ISBN 0-8144-5918-8

First hardcover edition. Originally
published by AMACOM in looseleaf
format © 1987 V. Clayton Sherman.

Printing number

20 19 18 17 16

For
Ann and Andrew,
who are,
and know how to make,
winners.

If you treat a man as he is, he will remain as he is. But if you treat him as if he were what he ought to be, and could be, he will become what he ought to be and could be.

—Goethe

You see, really and truly, apart from the things anyone can pick up, the difference between a lady and a flower girl is not how she behaves, but how she's treated. I shall always be a flower girl to Professor Higgins, because he always treats me as a flower girl, and always will; but I know I can be a lady to you, because you always treat me as a lady, and always will.

—Eliza Doolittle, in George Bernard Shaw's *Pygmalion*

Preface

Managing problem people is the most frustrating part of management. Employees who cannot or will not perform are so out of sync with the manager's own desire for achievement that they represent an almost insuperable communication problem. On top of the manager's daily work pressures is heaped the unwanted load of a few people who demand a disproportionate share of time and attention.

This manual is designed to help managers either solve these problems or rid their organization of people who will not respond.

For the first 11 years of my professional career, I wrestled with these issues as a practicing manager and human resources executive. As a problem arena, it is both legal and psychological, both policy and politics, both stress and mess.

And in the last ten years, I've had the opportunity to work on a consulting basis in over a thousand organizations and seen the universal nature of the problem. It cuts across all industries, job descriptions, ages, and educational levels. My client firms continually request assistance with the problem. What they all seek is a reference manual of techniques and specific approaches, not simply a discussion of the topic. Furthermore, executives made clear, give us a tool that isn't oriented toward just one approach; we need something pragmatic but not simplistic.

I believe that this book will be such a tool.

First, it is written for the practicing manager. While there are research bases for the conclusions and principles presented here, this book is primarily for the man or woman faced with the need for immediate, practical answers.

Second, this book can be thought of as a tool kit, stocked with a wide range of approaches and options, each of which can be effective when employed under the proper circumstances. For example, while counseling may be a useful tool with some problem employees, it is totally worthless with others. And so the text does not endorse one behavioral, psychological, or legal approach over any other.

In management, the prime question is, "Does it work?" Any craftsperson knows that you use different tools for different jobs. My aim has not been to tell manager craftspeople how to do their jobs, but to provide a clear picture of the tools available and when and how to use them.

An added feature is the Inventory on Problem Employee Managing (IPEM). In Chapter 3, a sample is given of the IPEM's three parts: the Inventory, the Answer and Discussion Booklet, and the Action Plan. Here the manager can determine his present knowledge level, quickly identify areas where additional knowledge is needed, and map out a specific plan of attack for dealing with problem cases. The book delivers!

Two other very useful tools are the Planned Performance forms, which allow a manager to exert very close control and perform a very detailed evaluation. The forms are displayed and discussed in Chapter 6. In essence, these represent a simple, but instantly usable, version of management by objectives.

I would like to point out to readers that I have frequently used the pronoun *he* to connote both genders. It should be emphasized, however, that this has been done solely in the interests of avoiding awkwardness and that such passages are of course intended to apply equally to both genders.

I am indebted to the many managers and executives who helped me understand this arena of management action, particularly in terms of how devastating to a business it can be if not dealt with. I'm grateful to them, too, for showing me the kind of courage and dedication to excellence that are necessary to really confront it.

I further want to acknowledge my debt to the many behavioral scientists and human resources professionals who have labored to bring forth the elements of applied leadership in organizational settings. A very special mention goes to Dr. Mark Silber, my friend, colleague, and mentor of 20 years. I would also like to remember my doctoral committee of long ago: Drs. Roger Wallace, Uldis Smidchens, and Gene Booker of Western Michigan University's Colleges of Business Administration and Education.

As a writer, my work has been substantially improved and polished by my kindly, curmudgeonly AMACOM editor, Adrienne Hickey, a master at getting greater performance by upping the standards and showing how.

This book is dedicated to my wife—and for good reason. She has provided the support, both professionally and personally, that really made this possible. It is dedicated, as well, to my son, Andrew, whose potential as a future president of the United States I am the first to predict.

Contents

1

From Losers to Winners

He was sent home from school with a note. As a fourth grader, he'd already been judged by his teacher as "incapable of learning." He couldn't concentrate, couldn't read well, couldn't keep up with others.

His mother had no choice — she would have to teach the nine-year-old. There were no other schools, no other sources of help. She vowed to prove the teacher wrong.

On their small farm was a windmill. Here she could curb her son's activity. Every day she took him to the top of it. There they'd read and talk and laugh. Sometimes there was an apple for a treat for a lesson mastered.

A windmill is a strange place to learn. Atop it, up high in the sky, your view extends for miles. For a small boy, intimidated and disparaged by an adult world, this look down on adult-sized barns and houses revealed them shrunken into smaller perspective. Maybe it even gave him a feeling of being on top of things.

Though his formal schooling did not go past this farm wife's effort of two seasons, it sufficed. It turned on his intellect, fired his imagination, made him confident and determined.

Later he would garner 1,137 patents, more of them than any person before or since. He would transform daily life for humanity by a greater degree and in more ways than any other scientist or inventor before or since. His discoveries would so astound the world and radically alter his times that he would come to be known as the Wizard of Menlo Park. Thomas Alva Edison, the grammar-school dropout, became one of the great ones. In turning failure into success, he went from loser to winner.

Seeing Negatives

It is one of the great recurring themes of life that many winners start out as losers. And it is one of the great challenges for anyone in a leadership role at work to be the one who makes this transformation happen in others' lives. The theme is so common, and is proved true so often, that one would think it could never be forgotten. Having evidence of the transformability of human lives so frequently before us, one would think that we would look at losers and automatically see winners. But the common response is otherwise. If we are irritated or annoyed by others, we do not see their capability or their potential — only the problem; we see only what they are not. It's a common — even, I suppose, normal — perceptual shortcoming that we focus on negatives.

But management is a positive game that's all about winning. Managers are paid to turn losing situations into winning performances. Their focus is not to suffer with what is, but to be transformers who change things and people into what they are capable of becoming.

Losing as a Basis for Winning

There are so many stories of the person brought low by failure who ultimately succeeds. What it is about difficulty, losing, and failure that breeds success? Certainly it doesn't work for everyone, but losing can be an inspiration for winning.

A key to understanding how this works is that failure sets up a *challenge environment*. Nobody gives palaces, pay increases, or promotions to losers. And if you want those things, you're going to have to pick yourself up off the ground and start doing what it takes to get them. Losing doesn't really reward us a whole lot — a fact that helps provide the impetus for breaking the failure cycle.

Sometimes the loser sets out to prove wrong the one who labeled him so. Take the story of one who was a hard charger. The energy was there, yes, and the talent, as well. But he pushed too hard. He annoyed; he irritated.

His early life was one of hard work and a poor home. It made him hungry and eager to fulfill his father's dreams. Later, in a corporate world, there was something about him that didn't seem to fit: He wasn't smooth enough, not polished the way some of the Ivy Leaguers were. At times, his forcefulness showed through, like a street fighter at a tea party.

The rough edges didn't matter much in the early career; they could be written off to brashness. But when he reached the upper levels, his ambition was such that he could smell the top spot. And the drive for it didn't set well with the Grosse Pointe set, particularly with his boss, an autocratic man who didn't like his judgment questioned.

I suppose it was inevitable, the termination. Yet the fall from grace was unexpected, the fall from power devastating. Most men could not have taken it. He was finished in the industry. Nobody, not even Humpty Dumpty, could put the pieces back together again. He was judged a loser that day, when Henry Ford II fired him — dismissed Lee Iacocca.

This "loser" went on to become a legendary symbol. The American spirit was low in those days of the Iranian hostage crisis and worldwide recession. Unemployment and organization failures were everywhere. The rebuilding of Chrysler became a symbol of something far greater than the value of a single corporation; it became a symbol of victory emerging from defeat, of a Phoenix spirit rising from the ashes. If it was possible to rebuild Chrysler, maybe it was possible to renew spirit and country.

Whether people should have given Iacocca so much credit was beside the point. The factual analysis that critics were poised to offer was silenced in a great release of national purpose. Not all of it was caused by the Chrysler story, surely, nor by the man who pulled success out of the hat like a rabbit, but it satisfied the hunger that millions of others felt, as well. It was the story of America, of the underdog who wins. It was our story.

In his own book, Lee Iacocca spoke candidly of his feelings about being labeled a loser by Mr. Ford. It became a great source of motivation, sparking his desire to rebuild Chrysler as a way of proving Henry wrong. Strange, isn't it, that the best decision Henry may ever have made was to brand Lee a loser?

Fighting the "Loser" Label

Sometimes losers are just too dumb to know they are losers; they don't understand that they're getting nowhere and ought to throw in the towel. The person who finally wins may have been counted out several times but didn't hear the referee! Certainly that was the case with one athlete. He wasn't a pretty fighter, nor elegant. He was a slugger, not a boxer. Often he would be knocked down because he didn't plant his feet right. His face bore the scars of many cuts because he carried his gloves too low. He did everything a fighter shouldn't do; his technique was so lackluster that it's a wonder he fought so many bouts.

On one occasion, a reporter remarked about how the fighter kept being knocked down. The classic reply gives real insight into how winners keep going when everybody says to quit: "It don't matter how many times they knock you down. What counts is how many times you get up." The words are those of Rocky Marciano, then heavyweight champion of the world.

Later the spirit of Rocky would be celebrated in the fictional exploits of Rocky Balboa. The sensational box office appeal of the *Rocky* films centers around the image of a loser who had nothing going for him except determination to be more that he was. Note how millions of people identified with the story. Was this attraction just coincidence or good marketing, or was it because the Rocky saga expressed a life theme that many found compelling?

The book *Rocky II* begins at the end of Rocky's first bout with Apollo Creed, the great champion. Rocky had no illusions about winning, but it was his great dream to " go the distance"—last 15 rounds with Apollo—something no other fighter had ever done. Sylvester Stallone gives Rocky these words:

This was it.

I was gonna be knocked out.

This is when all of them guys out there with their pencils, poundin' them typewriters, start writin' the word "bum" or "lucky," or "I knew he couldn't do it."

It was the quietest time of my life.

I didn't hear nobody yellin', I didn't hear no birds tweetin' inside my head, I didn't hear Mickey screamin'. I just looked across that wet spot, an' underneath the bottom rope I could see his mouth movin', his mouth was sayin', "Stay down."

He couldn't've been talkin' to me, because I had come here to stand up, not to stay down, and I knew if I didn't get up I was gonna hate myself for the rest of my life. As a matter of fact, that's what bothered me more than anythin'. I didn't care that people would say, "He's a nobody."

"He ain't nothin'."

"He couldn't go the distance."

"It was a lucky shot from South Philly."

That never bothered me. What bothered me was when I was gonna be alone, mebbe when I was fifty or sixty or ninety, and I'd look back an' say to myself, "Three more minutes, Rocky, three more; why couldn't you do it?" [1]

Sometimes the loser really is a loser, at that particular time and in that particular situation. But life has many seasons and many possibilities. The world spins on its axis, people change and grow, circumstances evolve. What goes around comes around.

Losing Puts Us in Touch

Losing, it is said, teaches you who your friends are. Anyone who's been through a divorce, an illness, the death of a loved one, knows that there is a lot of falsity in life — false friends, false values, false goals. Big houses and fancy cars are nice, but they don't really count.

It's important to understand that losers, whether problem employees or members of our own family, are often going through an intense and important learning experience. People who've been through the wringer report that they really sorted their priorities out, that they got "back in touch." Particularly, they got back in touch with:

1. *Themselves.* When the supports are knocked out by job loss, career or personal failure, or some great tragedy, it forces a reexamination of personal goals and objectives. We throw out a lot of excess baggage; we get the heft of things.

2. *Loved ones.* Failure causes us to realize that, if we're lucky, we might have a few people who really care for us. We come to appreciate and relate to these people in a new way. They become truly important to us. We tend to stop being so manipulative and become more genuine, caring, and deep.

3. *The future.* A little reminder of one's limitations and mortality can do wonders for behavior and character. The story of most people's maturation in the journey of life involves a movement toward better personal behavior and more important goals. Maybe it's just finally growing up, but getting smacked around by life sometimes helps.

In Shakespeare's *As You Like It*, the Duke has been banished from the court. He is in disgrace and exiled from his country. Only a few of his friends have stayed with him, but the cause is not lost because the young leader uses this negative experience, letting it teach and strengthen him:

> Sweet are the uses of adversity,
> Which like the toad, ugly and venomous,
> Wears yet a precious jewel [marking] in his head;
> And this our life, exempt from public haunt,
> Finds tongues in trees, books in the running brooks,
> Sermons in stones, and good in everything.[2]

Losing Releases Focusing Energies

From history comes the tale of a young boy who spoke poorly. The exact nature of his speech impediment is not entirely evident from the written record. Perhaps he stuttered or stammered. In any event, people made fun of him, and the sting of not fitting in, always painful for any adolescent, was made even more difficult for him by those who thought his handicap a punishment from the gods or an indication of a mental defect.

To overcome his shyness and withdrawn nature, he engaged in athletics, and to strengthen his faltering voice, he would go down to the edge of the ocean, where the waves crashed like thunder on the rocks, and shout out his frustration in speeches over the roar of the surf.

The boy filled his mouth with pebbles. His purpose: to force his tongue to form the words around them. He had to concentrate all his mental and physical energy on linking mind and tongue, on making the sounds articulate.

The lad, Demosthenes, became the greatest orator of ancient Greece. He turned his weakness into strength.

Psychologists refer to this as compensation. When we fail, a healthy defense mechanism is energized that makes us put more effort into other areas where we might be able to succeed or pushes us to try even harder in the area of our failure. Consider this example:

An eleven-year-old had a severe asthmatic condition and suffered a bout of childhood polio. The doctors said he would never walk again without assistance. What went through that child's mind we may never know, but the boy purposed in his heart that he would walk, that he would have a normal life.

He followed the exercise regimen prescribed for him but did 40 and 50 times the amount of exercises ordered. He worked at it obsessively, driven by his failure. He began lifting small weights, then added another pound or two. Little by little, his strength returned; the muscles grew. In 1956, Paul Anderson won the Olympic Gold Medal in weight lifting and went on to a fabulous professional career. His feats are still recalled, and many of his records remain unbroken. Weakness turned into strength.

What am I saying? That every kid with physical handicaps can win Olympic gold?

No, though I wish it were possible. What I am saying is that nobody can take it for granted that a kid with polio *can't* win Olympic gold. I'm saying that every loser you're dealing with at work might have the potential to be your boss or your boss's boss or to own the company! I'm saying that the minute we start writing people off, we're writing ourselves out of an opportunity to be a developer of greatness in others. I'm saying that when we close the door on people because they've only showed us their losing side, we cannot be a cocreator in their winning. I'm saying that this might be the greatest opportunity of your life to go down in the history books. You could be a savior of others.

Greater than the Great

In each of these cases of people rising to fame and glory, there is too great a tendency to depict them as something more than mere mortals, something beyond average human beings struggling to emerge. A cold analysis suggests otherwise. Adm. Bull Halsey, one of America's greatest heroes, who participated in the decisive Battle of Midway that broke the Japanese navy in 1942, wrote: "There are no great men. There are only ordinary men, forced by circumstances to greatness."

Think it through.

Despite how great some of us do become, I can't help but wonder about those who help losers make their transition to greatness. What of those who helped the famous ones cross the bridge from defeat to victory? I wish historians had paid more attention to them. This story is a case in point:

The setting was the frontier. Life was harsh, existence hand-to-mouth. The boy slept on hay or corn cobs to protect himself from the cold of the dirt floor. There were no welfare supplements, no comforts. There were no great museums, no cultural pursuits beyond some occasional fiddle playing. The only schooling available was the basic "readin', writin', and cipherin' to the rule of three."

Awkward and shy, the boy showed no special aptitude. His stepmother might have merely tolerated him until he could leave the house as a teenager. His moving on would make a little more food available for her own children. There was no reason for her to expect more from him than from her own. Certainly the wilderness society of the day expected nothing. He was just another farmer's kid, with no prospects, no chances.

However, the boy did show a curious interest in words: He'd scrawl them on a slate or in the dirt. And books: He liked to read the simple little stories from the ragged schoolbooks. It was a rare person who could read and write more than his name. To be interested in reading was to provoke derision among chums and siblings.

What kind of person was this stepmother, who shushed the other laughing children? Why, in a world whose sheer drudgery put people in an early grave, would this woman take in other people's laundry in order to buy the boy books from passing travelers? With her arthritic body, why walk miles just to borrow a book for her adopted son to read? As he lay sprawled on the floor poring over the latest treasure that she'd found, she would say to the others, wrestling noisily: "Hush, you leave Abe alone. Someday he's going to amount to somethin'."

Abe. Abe Lincoln. His name would be unknown without Sarah Bush Lincoln. So who really was greater? The one so ably launched, or the one who did the launching?

At work, some managers see people as they are and complain and become irritated. Others look at people and glimpse the opportunity to transform lives and build their business. In research done with company presidents into factors they look for in assessing a manager's promotability, they often spoke of the top prospects as people growers. The most promotable managers, they said were turnaround artists with people's lives —leaders who got mileage and results where others only saw problems and losers. I think it fair to say the evidence shows that leading problem people into the winner's circle is a significant factor in a manager's career ascent.

From the pages of *Harvard Business Review* comes the story of "Sweeney's miracle," a true-life example of how managerial commitment can change performance:

> James Sweeney taught industrial management and psychiatry at Tulane University, and he also was responsible for the operation of the Biomedical Computer Center there. Sweeney believed that he could teach even a poorly educated man to be a capable computer operator. George Johnson, a black man who was a former hospital porter, became janitor at the computer center; he was chosen by Sweeney to prove his conviction. In the morning, George Johnson performed his janitorial duties, and in the afternoon Sweeney taught him about computers.
>
> Johnson was learning a great deal about computers when someone at the university concluded that, to be a computer operator, one had to have a certain I.Q. score. Johnson was tested, and his I.Q. indicated that he would not be able to learn to type, much less operate a computer.
>
> But Sweeney was not convinced. He threatened to quit unless Johnson was permitted to learn to program and operate the computer. Sweeney prevailed, and he is still running the computer center. Johnson is now in charge of the main computer room and is responsible for training new employees to program and operate the computer.[3]

And here's the key point of the story: Sweeney's expectations were based on his belief in his own teaching ability, not on his belief in Johnson's learning credentials.

The Blessings of Losing

In part, losing is a test of character—a chance to see whether the loser has the ability to bounce back from defeat. For all of us, life has its share of losing, its defeats and pain that must be borne. It is these testing times that allow us to see others and ourselves most clearly. Does the loss disclose a resiliency, a bounce-back ability? In the face of a seemingly insurmountable obstacle, is there the dogged determination that tunnels through the mountain or devises ways to go around, over, or under it?

For years, Edison had sought a material suitable for use as a filament in the electric light bulb. He had tested all kinds of metals, natural fibers, and even his wife's sewing thread—literally over a thousand tries. Each filament was laboriously and painstakingly placed inside hand-blown glass bulbs and the air then extracted. Each failed. In an interview, Edison was asked: "How can you keep on? You've failed over a thousand times!" And Edison, completely taken aback, replied: "Failed! I haven't failed. I've successfully learned of 1,000 things that won't solve this problem."

Did you catch it? It isn't just thinking positive; it is an attitude that defines failure not as losing, but rather as *not yet having attained the goal.*

If we had the mind-set of an Edison, we would not see people who are failing at work as losers, but as people who have not yet attained the goal. I think that's the way a loving parent sees children, and it's that attitude that makes it possible to keep working with people who would otherwise try our patience. Just as it requires an unbelievable amount of maturity in the parent, so it requires patience and maturity in a work setting to deal with people who certainly have not attained the goal. I suspect managers' possession of this maturity qualifies them to lead problem people, while the absence of it probably disqualifies them.

Psychological studies show that we tend to underrate people more than we overrate them. We see others' faults more than we see their virtues. We judge them harshly for what they are not. Because they are not perfect, we fail to encourage them to be what they can become. In part, the evidence suggests that we tend to see ourselves critically, as well, and our faulty self-image then impairs our ability to see the greatness in other people.

Life Is a Kaleidoscope

Another common failing of managers is thinking that people are forever fixed — "What you see is what you get." But people, even "losers," are not fixed. We are like a kaleidoscope: When you change the viewing perspective, a whole new person is seen. We are different at age 25 from the way we were at 18. We are not the same people at 40 as we were at 30. People's potentials may or may not be great, but they are absolutely unknown to us. We simply cannot rate a person's potential. Who would have dreamed that the star of *Bedtime for Bonzo* could become president of the United States?!

As managers, we are pressured for results in so many areas — productivity, financial gain, customer service. There seems so little time left to deal with human relationships and the processes of behavior management. Yet studies indicate that truly effective leaders spend more time worrying about peoples' growth and retooling than they do in focusing on work concerns. They understand that management is "getting things done *through other people.*"

Ineffective managers focus on getting things done but don't hear that second phrase — "through other people." Such managers are the real losers and failures at work. Their job is to set the standards high and get people to shape up so that they turn in winning performances.

The Leper Colony

Allow me to share one final story. I was a direct observer and know that it's true. In my student days, I worked one summer for a company's school-equipment division, where we made school chairs and desks. The unit to which I was assigned was the "Leper Colony," so named because we had more misfits per square inch than anywhere else in the firm. The reason for this was that Mike Jensen, the supervisor, made a standing offer to all the other managers in the plant. Basically, his message was: "If you get fed up with some turkey and are ready to tie a can to his tail, send him to me. If I can't shape him up, I'll fire him for you and save you the trouble." Well, as you can imagine, managers were lined up down at the personnel department to get the transfer forms processed! The Leper Colony was a dumping ground for the rejects. (I hasten to add that the only reason I was assigned to the Leper Colony was that I was hired as a summer replacement!)

One noon hour I was eating my lunch behind a large packing case, where I was out of sight. The only person on the floor was the latest arrival at the Leper Colony, a gum-chewing, arrogant-looking, motorcycle-jacket-wearing, unshaven, walking attitude problem. He was the kind of guy who didn't just wear a cigarette pack rolled up in his shirt sleeve; he wore the whole carton!

Mike Jensen walked in. About 5′6″ tall and nearly that wide, he was so big that when he walked through the double doors, the air pressure in the room changed! Mike was not a pretty sight. A former navy man, he lacked college credentials. In fact, if you were to judge talent by appearance, you wouldn't figure this person as being capable of anything. Yet Mike Jensen was one of the greatest leaders I've ever met.

Mike walked over to greet the new reject. How did he approach him? Was there any discussion of positive expectations, of nice little training programs, or of Mike's desire to establish a warm personal relationship? No. Mike went up to him and, without a word, just reached out his massive arms, grabbed him by his leather lapels, and literally lifted him off the floor. The victim found himself hanging in midair as Mike slowly flexed his arms. Finally, still dangling this poor fish in the air, Mike said: "Everybody tells me I ought to can your rear end. I'm not going to make it that easy on you. Are you ready to grow up? Are you ready to be a man? Are you ready to do some work?"

Well, it was no Cinderella story, but the walking attitude problem stayed, and the problems were finally worked through.

One interesting sidelight to the story is the fact that the name "Leper Colony," originally used as a mark of ridicule and derision, came to be a source of pride. You see, our productivity exceeded that of all other units in the plant, and the label "Leper Colony" became a badge of honor, painted by the workers on the sides of their lunch buckets as a sign of pride.

Summary

Problem employees *can* be led, and they will respond. They can learn and change. They can catch a vision from leaders who are strong, competent, and able to motivate. But like the great growth masters who assist the famous, managers have to have their own vision, a commitment to growth, and the courage to try.

This manual presents several hundred specific suggestions, strategies, techniques, and tools. They will help, but by themselves they will not make winners out of losers. *You* will be responsible for the winning that takes place.

Will you succeed with every person? Probably not, and this book will show you how to get rid of those you can't count as successes. But you can succeed with a lot of people, and some will be the great ones — the ones you boost from losers to winners.

2

Who Is the Problem Employee?

The problem employee. It seems as if every manager has at least one. At conferences all over the country, I hear a continuing lament from men and women in leadership positions who are frustrated and troubled by their inability to get through to the employee who has become the departmental problem child, the pariah, the leper of the unit.

When groups of managers are asked to identify the kinds of problems these people present, a relatively long list emerges. It includes specific behavioral difficulties as well as those problems that seem primarily attitudinal or motivational.

Defining the Problem Employee

What are the *behavioral* problems that most managers report? Well, they involve the person with a high lost-time rate, the person who doesn't phone in to indicate he or she isn't going to make the shift. It's the continually tardy employee, the employee who drinks or takes drugs. It's the employee with continued financial or legal problems, the employee who creates accidents or seems to have more than his or her fair share of accidents, the rule breaker, the person with no confidence. And certainly it's the person whose work quantity or quality is below accepted levels.

What are some of the *attitudinal* or motivational problems that managers complain about? The insubordinate employee probably heads the list, or it could be the one who has a "bad attitude." It's the employee who undermines the boss with the work group, the employee who damages group morale, the continually complaining employee or the gossip monger who stirs people up, creating friction within the work group. In some cases, it's the stressed employee or the employee suffering mental-health problems.

In addition, at a recent seminar, supervisors listed the following problem types:

□ Lazy, apathetic, and pleasant-to-your-face unreliable employees
□ Time wasters, "bathroom hiders," and lunch lizards
□ Back stabbers, busybodies, and wedge drivers
□ Employees with too many outside interests
□ Consistently rude and socially disruptive types
□ Boss underminers, sometimes uncooperative informal leaders, and disloyal individuals
□ Change resisters and passive aggressives

The list is long and specific, and a bit depressing to contemplate!

One survey revealed that between 4 and 11 percent of supervisors report experiencing problems in their department *on a regular basis* with employees who had:

□ Serious personal/emotional problems
□ Trouble living with the rules and regulations
□ Patterns of lateness or absence

That range increased to 33 to 51 percent with the addition of supervisors who reported experiencing these problems at least *sometimes*.[1] So you're not alone.

My own experience in dealing with thousands of managers in corporate-sponsored programs on this topic suggests that about 90 percent of managers must deal with at least one problem employee at some time during each year.

One employee assistance program (EAP) found that the ratios of problem employee types referred to it looked like this:

□ Some 45 percent were alcoholics.
□ About 25 percent had mental-health or stress problems.
□ Another 13 percent were experiencing family difficulties.
□ Some 7 percent were drug or substance abusers.
□ A final 10 percent were having a potpourri of problems—legal, financial, and so on.

These percentages may not hold up from company to company, and it should be kept in mind that these cases were severe enough that they'd been referred to a corporate assistance program. Nonetheless, the figures are useful in suggesting the presence of underlying patterns and groupings that ought to be looked for at work.

I think it's helpful in understanding the problem employee to emphasize that we're dealing with approximately 10 percent of the workforce at any given moment. Another study suggests that as many as 20 to 25 percent of the workforce may be emotionally disturbed at any given time.[2] The numbers are a little hard to pin down because the problem often involves a continuing cycle, with some people coming into a problem period while others are leaving it (or the company!). Also, differences in work environments and job class can influence the numbers of people who are affected, along with such factors as how tolerant or supportive the corporate climate is. So the numbers move around a bit, but the bottom line is this: A majority of managers experience problems with a sizable minority of their employees, and this set of problems is rated by supervisors as among their most difficult to deal with.

When asked to list the toughest tasks of management, managers — to no one's surprise, I'm sure — rate terminating someone for lack of performance as the toughest. The second toughest task most frequently mentioned in discussion is disciplining an employee; and the third most difficult, conducting performance evaluation. There are other tough tasks, but it's interesting to note that the three most formidable challenges in management all surround this central question of how one handles the problem person. How do you evaluate performance and administer discipline, and if those two approaches don't work, how do you fire the misfit? This area of dealing with problem performance is the most difficult, most traumatic of management work.

Narrowing the Definition

Earlier I stated that problem employees represent approximately 10 percent of the workforce at any given time. To indicate the dimensions of the situation more precisely, that figure can be broken down. About half the 10 percent are the hard-core group, who will be difficult to save, and about half can be salvaged, turned around, or helped to adapt. In some cases, those who are salvaged will go on to become almost heroic figures within the organization, true superachievers and performers, and even role models for other employees. In other cases, they can be brought back only to an average level of acceptability or adequacy. The remaining 5 percent, or less than 5 percent in some organizations, are the hard nuts that nobody seems able to crack. This book will help you salvage the 5 percent that can be salvaged and, in some cases, give you new ideas for how to deal with that recalcitrant second 5 percent that so few can reach.

I think it has to be understood at the outset that you're not going to salvage everyone. As one manager said, "If Jesus Christ had Judas, and Washington had Benedict Arnold, I think you're entitled to at least one of these people." You're not going to get through to everybody.

My mother used to say that "some people's minds are like concrete — all mixed up and permanently set," and you're going to be dealing with some deep-rooted, and perhaps permanently set, behaviors. The employee's spouse might have been working on that same problem behavior, criticizing it, pushing it for the past 20 years. She hasn't been able to change it, and it's doubtful that you're going to change it. The employee himself may have made a real effort to change and hasn't been able to do it either. We must recognize the fact there are some people we're not going to be able to get through to, and those are the people who probably should be terminated from the organization. How to use that ultimate remedy will be discussed in Chapter 12.

A Vital Distinction

It's important to distinguish between the problem employee and the *problemed* employee. Given that troubles are such an integral part of life, all employees will one day experience problems. There will be financial difficulties or a divorce or the death of a loved one, and for a period of time, there is a dip in the employee's performance, or there is an unhappy person who seems to be snapping at everyone. Most managers learn that these short performance dips are temporary and this individual will come back strong, again giving his typically fine performance. All employees are at one time or another problemed people. The appropriate course of treatment is to be supportive, be a counselor, be a friend. Be there to listen and perhaps refer the individual to other sources of help inside or outside the organization. These people will bounce back and regain their ability to contribute.

But in the case of the truly problem person, we're dealing with someone whose problems seem more intense, deeper, and certainly longer-lasting. We seem to see a continuing inappropriateness in what the individual does and says. When the supervisor offers support or issues a reprimand or provides counsel, he finds that the employee does not respond, does not seem to have the capability or understanding to snap out of this troubled behavior.

In this book, we are focusing primarily on the situation caused by the truly problem employee and not simply a temporarily problemed one.

Who's to Blame?

In considering what constitutes a problem employee, it is important to note that we are dealing with a problem cause or fault that rests primarily with the employee and not with the manager. In one study of employees who were brought to the attention of corporate personnel departments by their complaining managers, it was determined that about half the cases really reflected problem management rather than problem employees. That is, some supervisors would run off to the personnel department and use it as a club against the employee. The reality, in the political world of organizational living, is that if there is a conflict between employee and manager, the manager's greater power, status, and credibility can subvert or overrule the employee. It is a fact that managers can make employees look bad and appear responsible for problems that may be rooted in poor supervisory practices. The study found that about half the employees who were labeled as problem people by their managers were in fact the victims of a manager who had not provided adequate training, counseling, or written warnings or lacked personal patience or a belief in his ability to develop others. And so, when there was difficulty with a particular employee, the employee tended to get blamed or fired.

Every organization has to recognize the fact that not all of its managers walk on water and that even the best executives sometimes foul up their people dealings. This manual makes no attempt to present all the knowledge that goes into good supervisory practices and good management but is limited to a discussion of those cases where the real trouble lies with employee malperformance.

Costs of the Problem Employee

Why should we take action against the misfits? Well, I guess because they cost so much. One EAP administrator found that in his *Fortune* 500 company, the following costs are incurred by problem employees:

- The problem employee typically has a lost-time rate six times higher than a member of the nonproblem group and is a more frequent claimer on medical insurance.
- The problem employee is a more frequent and heavier user of workers' compensation. Aetna reported that in its own experience, the problem employee was 60 percent more likely to have an accident than an average employee and a first-time claimant had a 40 percent chance of repeating.
- The problem employee exhibits lower productivity, the average output of the problem person being about two-thirds that of the average employee.
- The problem employee is four times more likely to be an alcoholic than is a member of the acceptably performing employee group.

There are additional major cost factors. Problem employees, as a group, are more likely to make poor decisions, and if proper corrective action is not taken, they can increase the turnover among good employees, who get fed up with the misfits' increasingly negative influence. A terrific cost is paid in terms of loss of group morale and loss of the group's respect for its manager. Surveyed employees will often complain that they do not understand why management takes no action against people in their work group who are not really part of the team.

A lot has been written about the damage done by the problem employee to group morale, but a factor that I've seen almost no mention of is the damage such an employee causes to management morale. Managers just get so frustrated and feel such a loss of confidence because they can't solve these problems that it begins to erode their sense of confidence and mastery in other aspects of the job. Leaders start to falter or start to feel that they are failing. I think that can't help but permeate the work unit.

A very substantial amount of management time is invested in these people, time that others desperately need to deal with far more important problems, such as satisfying customers' needs and improving product quality. While problem employees and problemed employees represent an estimated 10 percent of the workforce at any given time, managers report that they will spend as much as 50 percent of their employee communication time in the work unit with these people. That means that the 90 percent of the people who are at least acceptable performers are only going to get 50 percent of the manager's available communication time. And so, the manager will feel guilty about not giving as much attention to the troops as he would like.

Other costs include theft, sabotage, industrial espionage, and even loss of organizational momentum.

The costs generated by the problem employee were detailed by a number of frustrated managers at a recent conference. Note how specific their list is and how it amplifies some of the points already made:

- Other workers become hostile toward the problem employee, with a resultant falloff in cooperation with him.
- Word of mouth spreads quickly, causing problems recruiting fresh talent into the unit — nobody wants to work with this person.
- Wastage of resources causes a slowdown in getting projects out, which in turn leads to unhappy executives. The scenario was described by one manager as akin to "a dirty snowball rolling downhill." Another described it as a "domino effect."
- Customer relations are damaged, as is the unit's image.
- Complications result when decision making, scheduling, and other procedures have to be changed to work around the problem person.
- On a political and motivational level, the problem employee cancels out the good things that happen and the successes that are achieved.
- Additional costs are created in other departments, either because of work foul-ups or because staff time is being expended — for example, in the personnel department. In turn, this creates interdepartmental friction.
- Increased training costs are generated, as well as increased legal liability.
- A number of managers believe that it increases turnover among good employees when problem employees are tolerated.
- Work standards are eroded and tend to decline.
- Creativity and initiative drop off among other employees.
- Fewer dollars are available to reward effective performers.

These and the other costs that problem people generate can be estimated in terms of dollars. Some of these costs can be accurately measured; in other cases, they can only be approximated. But if you add up all these confirmed costs and estimated costs, you might conclude, as one company did, that the costs its small group of problem employees represented were equivalent to 25 percent of payroll! That is, while the firm estimated its hard-core problem employee group to be about 3 percent of the head count and direct payroll, when all the costs generated by that 3 percent were added up, the total was equivalent to 25 percent of the annual payroll. In other words, these people generate a cost to the organization that is out of all proportion to their numbers. And the basic hard question that any management has to ask itseif is whether it can afford these people. Can *you* afford these people? Can you continue to live with the financial drag and the hassles they represent in your business?

Deciding to Take Action

It's been my experience that most managements that really crystallize the question like that do confront it. They come to the unpleasant conclusion that they have to clean house, that they must no longer tolerate the sloppiness these people represent and the damage they inflict. Managements then move to damage control, to a containment of these costs. If you work in a larger organization, you may find that the cost of these problems is staggering, almost astronomical. General Motors has estimated that alcoholism alone costs it in excess of $62 million a year.

Other organizations, while they may be motivated by the cost argument to take action, are also motivated by a remembrance of their own organizational mission and corporate values. Firms that are truly involved in the search for excellence and are acutely aware of the competitive realities of business in the closing decades of the twentieth century know that they have a responsibility to their human resources to call them to a higher level of performance and to reject standards that might have been tolerated in a less demanding era. We cannot have it both ways. We cannot be an excellent organization with mediocre people. We cannot be a strong and effective organization with weak and ineffective people. So a company's management must choose which it wants.

Our motivations are pure. We're not interested in hurting people or punishing people; we are interested in achieving worthwhile objectives. We are interested, too, in challenging people in such a way that they will want to change their behavior in order to accompany us on an exciting and positive journey.

Summary

Every manager is bound to have his fair share of problem employees: the lazy, the uncooperative, the emotionally unstable, the chronically late, the substance abusers — in short, workers who display one or more of a wide array of negative behaviors and attitudes.

What are a manager's chances of having to deal with such an employee? An informed estimate puts the chances at about nine out of ten. And how many employees typically fall into the problem category? Ten percent, in my experience — of which about half are, with effective managerial leadership, potentially salvageable; the other half comprise the hard-core group that may ultimately resist even the most concerted rehabilitative efforts.

In identifying problem employees, a couple of important distinctions must be made. The first is between the problem employee and the problemed employee — between the worker who habitually causes problems and the worker who happens to be experiencing pressures, stresses, or difficulties whose effects may be manifested in a temporary display of negative behavior or attitudes. Determining whether the troublemaker is a problem employee or a problemed employee will significantly affect how the manager confronts the issue. The second distinction that must be made involves correctly identifying the source of the problems. Some "problem employee" cases can, upon closer examination, disclose underlying supervisory or managerial shortcomings. The root cause must be accurately assessed before the trouble can be effectively managed.

The costs of problem employees include lower productivity, higher lost-time rates, increased use of workers' compensation, disproportionate demands on managerial time, damaged morale that can ultimately increase turnover, and on and on. What it all boils down to is dollars and cents, and standards. It is in fact possible for a firm's management to develop a good ballpark estimate of the financial drain occasioned by its misfit workers. The shock of this bottom-line figure is what very often prompts management to undertake a concerted damage-control effort.

3

Inventory and Action Plan for Problem Employee Managing

The Inventory on Problem Employee Managing (IPEM) is designed to increase management skills in dealing with problem people. It can be used either as a self-study tool or as an adjunct to a group seminar. The IPEM consists of three parts:

- □ A 56-item inventory, or self-assessment questionnaire, which allows the reader to examine his own current knowledge and attitudes. (See page 24.)
- □ An Answer and Discussion Booklet, for reference after the inventory has been completed. (See page 29.)
- □ An Action Plan, to map out steps the manager should take to deal with a particular problem employee. (See page 33.)

The IPEM questionnaire measures eight categories:

    I. Problem Dimensions
   II. The Manager's Role
  III. Positive Prevention
  IV. Counseling & Appraisal
   V. Positive Discipline
  VI. Special Cases
 VII. Disciplinary Procedures
VIII. Employee Termination

Ways to Use the Inventory

The following subsections provide a brief overview of some of the ways in which the IPEM instrument can be utilized as a tool for managing problem employees.

As a Self-Auditing Instrument

Managers can employ the IPEM to determine their level of knowledge. Often this is useful as part of an overall effort to deal with a current problem employee case — it helps managers "brush up" on what needs doing and sensitizes them to key issues.

As a Measure of Training Needs

IPEM response totals for each of the eight categories can be analyzed to identify areas that must be addressed through training programs. Since all categories have the same number of questions, it is easy to compare category scores, identify the lowest category scores, and plan program content accordingly.

Item analysis on individual questions is possible if particular management practices are to be audited prior to training. IPEM scores can also be compared to the norms provided to help determine the management team's overall proficiency in light of scores obtained in other organizations.

As a Seminar Discussion Generator and Educational Tool

Group discussions can be very fruitful. Shared responses are reinforcing and may result in group-specific ideas for problem employee management. Used as an educational tool, the inventory content increases awareness, provides a baseline for future score comparisons, and conceptually organizes and summarizes much of the knowledge base.

The IPEM can be used in group discussion in at least two other ways:

1. Category averages can be calculated for the group as a whole and the lower-rated categories then assigned to manager discussion groups. Such groups have been able to quickly diagnose problem areas and offer suggestions for their peers.
2. Those questionnaire items that are of particular interest to your own organization can be selected for discussion.

As a Post-Training Measure of Performance Change

The IPEM can be used in the conventional pretraining versus post-training manner, which is designed to measure knowledge gain during a training session. Total scores, category scores, or item scores on critical questions can be the basis for post-training measurement. (*Note:* Post-training measurement will be meaningless unless the seminar content has been directed to the content items covered in the IPEM.)

As a Tool for Management Coaching

It has been found that where individual coaching (either from a training person or from a supervisor) follows management education, the impact and application of that training will be greater. The IPEM may reveal areas of managerial knowledge, practices, or attitudes that need correcting or amplification. The IPEM should not be used as a performance evaluation instrument in a negative sense, but rather as the basis for open and helpful communication and counseling for future performance.

Administration

If you are using the IPEM with a group, you should tell participants that the purpose of the inventory is to allow them to take stock of their current knowledge of how to manage the problem employee. Participation should be voluntary and confidential.

Instructions provided on the cover of the IPEM instrument are concise and self-explanatory. It takes approximately 10 to 15 minutes to complete the IPEM, and participants should be allowed to complete it at their own rate. A pencil or ballpoint pen should be used in order to mark cleanly through the carbon paper.

Following scoring of the IPEM (discussed in the next section), read — and have other participants read — the Answer and Discussion Booklet, looking particularly at those items missed. These represent areas of possible knowledge gain.

Scoring

Open the IPEM and follow the scoring instructions as they appear inside. The test yields eight category scores and a total score. These raw scores should be entered in the first scoring-column row. The raw scores can then be rank-ordered, from highest-scoring category (1) to lowest-scoring category (8), and entered in the second scoring-column row. These raw scores and ranks can be compared with averages calculated for the group, if there is one, or with the national norms (see the following section), or both. Again, these norm scores and their ranks should be entered in the last two scoring-column rows.

Norms

The IPEM was first published in 1986, and the norms determined to date are preliminary. Average scores can be expected to vary by occupational group and industry. These preliminary norms presented here are for a general management population comprised of leaders from all hierarchy levels. First-line supervisory scores at the time of this writing seem to be somewhat lower than those obtained for middle or upper management.

	Category	Average Score	Rank
I.	Problem Dimensions	5.6	3
II.	The Manager's Role	6.2	1
III.	Positive Prevention	6.0	2
IV.	Counseling & Appraisal	4.3	7
V.	Positive Discipline	5.3	5
VI.	Special Cases	3.5	8
VII.	Disciplinary Procedures	5.4	4
VIII.	Employee Termination	4.7	6
	TOTAL	41.0	

In addition to the norms listed above, it is very useful for administrators to calculate averages for their participant groups. These peer-group norms are often more meaningful in helping individual managers assess how well they're doing. In calculating group norms, it is recommended that category averages as well as the average of total scores be determined. A format for displaying this information might look like this:

Category Scores

Participant	I.	II.	III.	IV.	V.	VI.	VII.	VIII.	TOTAL
1.									
2.									
3.									

Total the scores in each column. Then divide the totals by the number of scores in each column to get the arithmetical average.

Action Planning

Finally, when you're ready to proceed with the analysis of a particular problem case you're dealing with, complete the IPEM Action Plan. You may want to read through this manual first to pick up a number of pointers. But if you need the value of the Action Plan now, go to it!

The Forms

Copies of all three IPEM forms are shown starting on page 24. If you wish to use the Inventory, place a sheet of carbon paper between pages 26 (blank) and 27. *Do not* flip the paper over when you answer the questions on page 28. You can order copies of the Inventory (which are printed on special paper and do not require a carbon) and the other forms displayed in this book by writing to Dr. V. Clayton Sherman, c/o AMACOM Books, 135 West 50th Street, New York, New York 10020.

Summary

The Inventory on Problem Employee Managing, together with the Answer and Discussion Booklet and the Action Plan, are designed as practical tools for the management of problem employees. They can help the manager organize and analyze the information he already has about a given situation and the actions that have been taken to date. It can also help the manager pinpoint areas where obtaining further information or taking additional action might prove useful.

Other uses of the forms include assessing training needs, stimulating group discussions, measuring performance changes resulting from training, and management coaching.

Considerable insight into the management of problem employees can be gained by comparing each individual's IPEM category scores and total score with the averages calculated for the group as well as by comparing individual scores and group averages with the national norms.

Armed with the IPEM information, the manager can take effective action designed both to prevent the development of future problem employees and to minimize potential damage from existing problem employees, as will be discussed in the following chapters.

Inventory
on
Problem Employee
Managing
(IPEM)

Dr. V. Clayton Sherman

INSTRUCTIONS

Managing the problem employee is one of the most difficult tasks that managers face. This inventory will help you gain a better understanding of what alternatives are available and what limitations have to be managed around. Also, the instrument will help you create an Action Plan for what needs to be done if you currently have a case you're working on.

On the following pages you'll encounter 56 questions to help you assess your current knowledge of this important management subject. For each statement, you are asked whether you Agree [A] or Disagree [DA]. If you feel ambivalent, choose the response that is closest to your primary feeling about the subject.

Be sure to mark an answer for each statement by placing an "X" in the box that most nearly describes how you feel. If you wish to change your answer, draw a circle around the first "X" and mark a new "X" in the other box.

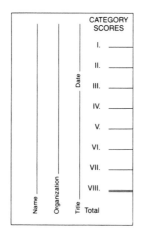

Examples:

12. Approximately half of the problem employees who should be terminated are never acted on because management is reluctant or afraid to take action. ☒ A ☐ DA

21. Self discipline is the most effective kind because it is internal and voluntary. ☒ A ☐ DA

Additional copies are available. For information, write to Dr. V. Clayton Sherman, c/o AMACOM Books, 135 W. 50th St., New York, NY 10020.

24

1. Problem employees represent only 3% of most organizations' work force, but they represent costs to the organization equivalent to 25% of payroll (lost time, lowered productivity, manager time, workmen's comp, medical costs).   [A] [DA]

2. At any one time, approximately one third to half of all supervisors report having problems with people who have deep personal or emotional difficulties, patterns of lateness or absence, or trouble living with the rules at work.   [A] [DA]

3. Average output of the problem person is about 2/3 of the average employee.   [A] [DA]

4. The Aetna reports that a problem employee is 60% more likely to have an accident than the average employee.   [A] [DA]

5. As a group, problem employees are four times more likely to be alcoholic than those who are acceptably performing.   [A] [DA]

6. The problem employee has a lost time rate 6 times higher than the average non-problem employee.   [A] [DA]

7. Most failures to meet work output requirements are caused by personality conflicts, personal problems, or poor attitudes.   [A] [DA]

8. Surveys indicate that managers rate their 3 toughest tasks as performance appraisal, employee discipline, and termination.   [A] [DA]

9. About half of the situations in which a problem employee is brought to the attention of Personnel are in reality caused by problem supervisors who have failed to perform their function.   [A] [DA]

10. New employees should be assigned to an organization's best managers because "winners make winners".   [A] [DA]

11. It is possible to tolerate mediocre and problem employees and still maintain an excellent organization.   [A] [DA]

12. Approximately half of the problem employees who should be terminated are never acted on because management is reluctant or afraid to take action.   [A] [DA]

13. Supervisory training and management development costs should not be viewed as an investment in terms of controlling problem employee costs.   [A] [DA]

14. It's been found that formal disciplinary procedures are unnecessary when excellent, well trained managers deal with people in the correct way.   [A] [DA]

15. It's easier, cheaper, less time consuming, and more productive to spend a lot of effort on employee selection than on getting people removed from the organization.   [A] [DA]

16. Organizations that fail to orient new employees are in danger of having their employees actually change the standards of the company.   [A] [DA]

17. In order to avoid problems, employees should not be used to the limits of their ability, given increasingly bigger jobs, or stretched to do more.   [A] [DA]

18. Organizations create employee animosity and distance from management by focusing on disciplinary procedures and quasi-legal approaches.   [A] [DA]

19. Organizations create a lot of negative employee reactions and confusion simply because they do not systematically reinforce or recognize good behaviors.   [A] [DA]

20. Career planning, job posting, career ladders, and job growth opportunities, while good things, have not been found to prevent problem employee behaviors.   [A] [DA]

21. Self discipline is the most effective kind because it is internal and voluntary.   [A] [DA]

22. Counseling and communication efforts are not appropriate in certain cases. If employees don't respond after two or three such attempts, it is quite likely that they will not do so, and other courses of action should be tried.   [A] [DA]

23. A coaching, teaching, parental approach has a greater probability of working than an authoritarian chewing out.   [A] [DA]

24. Research indicates that supervisors have a better chance of changing employee behavior by arranging consequences than by relying on communications for cases that are deepseated.   [A] [DA]

25. The counseling approach that has the greatest chance of working with the employee in terms of changing behavior is for the supervisor to ask a series of questions and listen intently for answers, guiding the employee to talk through problems.   [A] [DA]

26. When employees rate their own performance, they try to get away with a higher rating than they deserve, are not very honest in reporting their shortcomings, and feel less open to making changes in their behavior.   [A] [DA]

27. Supervisory performance ratings have been found to be largely invalid, often not legally defensible, and probably one of the biggest wastes of management time in industry today.   [A] [DA]

28. Performance appraisal should primarily be used to plan for employee development and target "where do we go from here" in work performance.   [A] [DA]

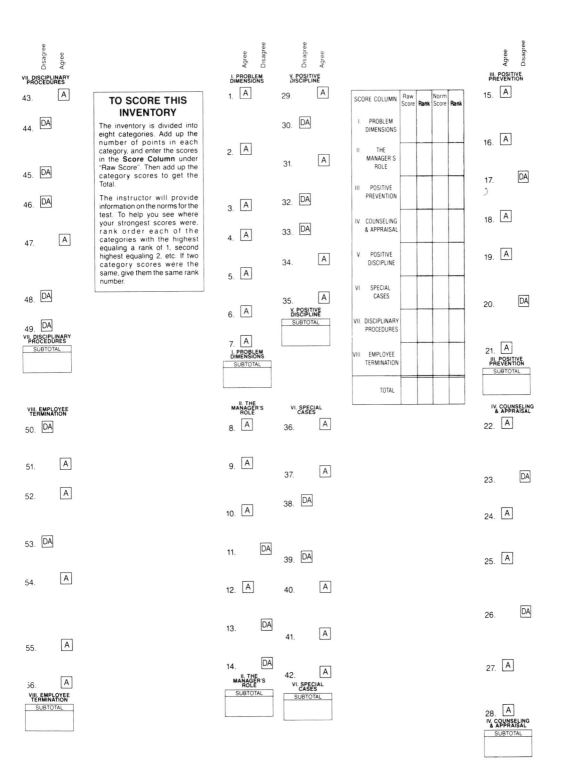

VII. DISCIPLINARY PROCEDURES

Disagree / Agree

43. A
44. DA
45. DA
46. DA
47. A
48. DA
49. DA

VII. DISCIPLINARY PROCEDURES
SUBTOTAL

VIII. EMPLOYEE TERMINATION

50. DA
51. A
52. A
53. DA
54. A
55. A
56. A

VIII. EMPLOYEE TERMINATION
SUBTOTAL

TO SCORE THIS INVENTORY

The inventory is divided into eight categories. Add up the number of points in each category, and enter the scores in the **Score Column** under "Raw Score". Then add up the category scores to get the Total.

The instructor will provide information on the norms for the test. To help you see where your strongest scores were, rank order each of the categories with the highest equaling a rank of 1, second highest equaling 2, etc. If two category scores were the same, give them the same rank number.

I. PROBLEM DIMENSIONS

Agree / Disagree

1. A
2. A
3. A
4. A
5. A
6. A
7. A

I. PROBLEM DIMENSIONS
SUBTOTAL

II. THE MANAGER'S ROLE

8. A
9. A
10. A
11. DA
12. A
13. DA
14. DA

II. THE MANAGER'S ROLE
SUBTOTAL

V. POSITIVE DISCIPLINE

Disagree / Agree

29. A
30. DA
31. A
32. DA
33. DA
34. A
35. A

V. POSITIVE DISCIPLINE
SUBTOTAL

VI. SPECIAL CASES

36. A
37. A
38. DA
39. DA
40. A
41. A
42. A

VI. SPECIAL CASES
SUBTOTAL

SCORE COLUMN	Raw Score	Rank	Norm Score	Rank
I. PROBLEM DIMENSIONS				
II. THE MANAGER'S ROLE				
III. POSITIVE PREVENTION				
IV. COUNSELING & APPRAISAL				
V. POSITIVE DISCIPLINE				
VI. SPECIAL CASES				
VII. DISCIPLINARY PROCEDURES				
VIII. EMPLOYEE TERMINATION				
TOTAL				

III. POSITIVE PREVENTION

Agree / Disagree

15. A
16. A
17. DA
18. A
19. A
20. DA
21. A

III. POSITIVE PREVENTION
SUBTOTAL

IV. COUNSELING & APPRAISAL

22. A
23. DA
24. A
25. A
26. DA
27. A
28. A

IV. COUNSELING & APPRAISAL
SUBTOTAL

29. Many supervisors overreact and try to change marginal behaviors that aren't worth changing. [A] [DA]

30. The supervisor should not let the employee know that he is documenting and creating a file in regard to problem behavior. [A] [DA]

31. When an employee's problems are discussed in a counseling session, the supervisor should also discuss the employee's positive behaviors. [A] [DA]

32. Personnel executives tend to be too conservative and make it all but impossible to fire poor performers. [A] [DA]

33. Punishments, such as layoffs, are usually effective in turning people around. [A] [DA]

34. If an employee maintains perfect behavior for an agreed upon period of time, his past disciplinary record should be removed. [A] [DA]

35. "Three times and out" is a reasonably good rule of thumb for the number of chances employees should be given to improve. [A] [DA]

43. Since so few employees are truly disruptive, formal disciplinary rules are not necessary. [A] [DA]

44. It's better to have a lot of specific rules to cover as many situations as possible, rather than just a few, so that employees don't make mistakes out of ignorance. [A] [DA]

45. A rule that is violated but never enforced is no longer a rule that can be enforced. [A] [DA]

46. In order for formal discipline to work, there must be a series of at least 4 warnings and an appeal avenue outside the direct chain of command. [A] [DA]

47. An effective approach to behavior control is a written and signed performance contract where the behavior that should occur is spelled out, along with review dates, conditions necessary for support, and standards of performance. [A] [DA]

48. Employees with poor performance records can be given a more severe penalty than is usually given. [A] [DA]

49. Discipline maintenance is a negative part of the supervisor's job. [A] [DA]

36. Managers should be looking for extremes of personality, stress symptoms, and people who seem out of control—these are the most common signs of mental disturbance. [A] [DA]

37. It's harder to correct a personal conduct problem than it is to deal with a job performance problem. [A] [DA]

38. Attendance will not improve simply by defining the rules, consistently applying penalties to absentees, keeping accurate records to single out the excessive absentee, and discussing reasons for absence. [A] [DA]

39. Alcoholics are more likely to be absent on Monday or Friday. [A] [DA]

40. Alcoholics and drug users respond best to "constructive coercion" where suspension or termination are threatened if the employee does not change his behavior. [A] [DA]

41. Drug users are more likely to be found in temporary jobs or lower skill level jobs than they have the capability to handle. [A] [DA]

42. There is a greater probability that the accident victim at work is suffering a mental illness than the employee who is accident-free. [A] [DA]

50. It is humane and caring to keep poor performers in jobs that they can't do, rather than terminating them. [A] [DA]

51. People should be fired so they can be successful someplace else. [A] [DA]

52. Actions leading to termination should be started as soon as it's clear that the employee has not responded to positive and negative disciplinary efforts. [A] [DA]

53. If an offense requires suspension or termination, it's best to wait until the end of the day or some other quiet time, such as lunch hour. [A] [DA]

54. The law, as a general principle, allows an employer to discipline or terminate an employee for any reason, good, bad or indifferent, as long as: 1) it is not prohibited specifically by law (as in discrimination cases), or, 2) it is not directed at an employee covered under a contract. [A] [DA]

55. The courts will support a decision to fire an employee even without documentation or evidence of step-by-step due process. [A] [DA]

56. In spite of technical failings or deficiencies in an employer's case, the court will primarily base its decision on three questions: 1) Did the employer deal fairly with the employee? 2) Was the process that led to termination objective? 3) Is there evidence of consistency in this case compared to others? [A] [DA]

Answer and Discussion Booklet

INVENTORY ON
PROBLEM EMPLOYEE MANAGING
(IPEM)

Dr. V. Clayton Sherman

INSTRUCTIONS

The following answers and discussion are meant to enlarge the point made in each of the questions in the Inventory on Problem Employee Managing. As you read the discussion items, look particularly at the answers for items that you missed in the Inventory.

Additional copies are available. For information, write to Dr. V. Clayton Sherman, c/o AMACOM Books, 135 W. 50th St., New York, NY 10020.

I. PROBLEM DIMENSIONS

1. **A.** Can you afford these people? Their cost is out of all proportion to their share of payroll. Either rehabilitate them or get rid of them.

2. **A.** These are the three most frequent problems supervisors report, although not necessarily the most difficult.

3. **A.** In part, this is caused by the amount of time problem employees spend off the job, in part by general performance malaise.

4. **A.** Problem employees tend to live out a sequence of problems, one after the other, including safety violations. That's one reason it's important to take corrective action early, rather than waiting for other problems to begin.

5. **A.** Read this question carefully. Problem employees are not all alcoholics, and many alcoholics are able to perform without being a problem. But if you spot a problem employee, there is a greater probability that he might be an alcoholic, and that his poor behavior is a symptom of alcoholism.

6. **A.** Lost time is a remarkably good indicator that deeper problems are operating. Never assume that the employee only has an attendance problem.

7. **A.** Incompetence and lack of job skills account for only a minority of problem employees.

II. THE MANAGER'S ROLE

8. **A.** Other "tough tasks" include work pressures and deadlines, organization politics, inadequate resources, etc. Note that the three toughest tasks all fall into the problem employee arena.

9. **A.** By failing to select people carefully, set performance expectations, communicate adequately, recognize achievement, and do the other positive things a good supervisor must do, supervisors set their people up for failure. A supervisor who complains about having a lot of problem people is usually the problem source.

10. **A.** Getting people "in the groove" is often simplest and best done by setting a good managerial example before their eyes. Research finds that managers who set high expectations get higher performance out of employees. If new employees are assigned to average supervisors, their later performance is likely to be only average.

11. **DA.** The rotten apple may not spoil the barrel, but that's the way to bet. Group morale tends to decline, and new employees particularly may start to pick up on poor behaviors seen in the problem person.

12. **A.** Because the task is sometimes disagreeable, and they lack sure knowledge of how to proceed, some managers fail to take action. What follows is a likely spreading of this problem. Sometimes this is found in a unit where a new manager inherits the dregs of past problems which his predecessor has passed on.

13. **DA.** Managers who have been trained in problem employee handling skills are better able to deal with the problem employee situation. Feeling more competent, they have more confidence, and tend to get better results. Management development has been found to be an investment that reduces costs caused by problem employees.

14. **DA.** No matter how good the manager, there's always somebody who can't figure it out. Disciplinary procedures are a tool providing an effective framework for dealing with people who weren't wise enough to benefit from a good supervisor.

III. POSITIVE PREVENTION

15. **A.** Sometimes organizations hire good people who later go sour. More often, people are hired who were problems the day they walked in the door. Managers trained in interviewing and selection, multiple interviews and interviewers, and formal assessment procedures all improve the chances of hiring winners instead of losers. While these approaches require a good deal of work, it's much less work, and it's more pleasant work than trying to get rid of problem people. Yet most organizations still spend relatively much less time on selection than they do on correction.

16. **A.** Given the increasing mobility and shortening employment spans of workers, it becomes imperative that people learn the expectations and culture of their employer. Organizations that don't manage this process have found that the attitudes and beliefs of strangers hired off the street have so changed the corporate atmosphere that it becomes an impossible situation to manage. Intensive orientation of 1-4 weeks costs less than the dollars spent in getting rid of a few problem employees and rehabilitating others.

17. **DA.** While it's true that people ought to be placed in jobs that are at their approximate level of ability to perform, it is a mistake to pigeonhole them there forever. One of the great keys of motivation is to continually stretch people, and increase their capabilities by pushing them.

18. **A.** Problems occur when the focus is primarily on policy rather than on people. Organizations should deal first with people's genuine needs for support, then turn to the disciplinary tools. In some organizations, the whole focus is to think in terms of appeal steps, grievances, writing people up, and the like; at that point the whole human relations climate runs downhill.

19. **A.** The single most frequent comment on attitude surveys is, "The only time you hear anything from management around here is when you do something wrong". From early childhood on, most people have encountered sources of systematic reinforcement for doing right. Parents, teachers, friends set up a conditioned expectation for recognition or praise for performance. Then we grow up, go to work, and it all stops! Result: confusion, animosity, suspicion, paranoia, and problems on the job.

20. **DA.** In addition to better job placement and growth of human assets, career management devices prevent a lot of frustration and steam build-up.

21. **A.** Managers cannot effectively supervise or control people by external control. Employees must be brought to a point where they desire to perform correctly. This requires that orientation and training, a positive work environment, good supervision, and all the aspects of a healthy environment are in place. It has been said that the desire to perform well is the whole definition of self-discipline.

IV. COUNSELING & APPRAISAL

22. **A.** Counseling is not a panacea. Emotionally disturbed employees who do not respond to counseling after two attempts should be referred to a professional. Some cases might respond to a layoff or other strategy. Part of good judgment in management is to not spend too much time beating a dead horse. If counseling doesn't work, try something else.

23. **DA.** This is one of those questions where the answer is, "it depends". Whether communication style is hard or soft depends in part on the personality you're dealing with. It also depends on what the current situation requirements are and what the past communication effort has been. A good rule of thumb is to say it nicely first, but then say it forcefully if you have to. Communications is a pragmatic art—do what works.

24. **A.** Modifying reward contingencies or payoffs is generally a far more powerful approach than continued counseling. A missed salary increase is more powerful than a pronoun; being uninvited to a social gathering is more powerful than a verb; being laid off with loss of pay is more powerful than a ton of paragraphs. Words are never a substitute for action.

25. **A.** This questioning-listening approach allows the manager to get a lot more information than a telling-selling approach. Its first benefit is diagnosis and greater control. The second gain comes in having the employee talk long enough through a series of questions that he begins to see possible solutions for his problem. At this point, there is usually better buy-in by the employee—it's his solution, not yours.

26. **DA.** The usual pattern is that about 90% of employees will rate themselves at or below the level where their supervisor would have rated them. For this reason an increasing number of organizations are turning to self evaluation as an approach to performance appraisal. The supervisor, of course, still reviews the rating, discusses it with the employee, and has the last say. Of the 10% who rate themselves higher than their boss would have rated them, about half do so in innocence, and they need to understand where they really are in their performance. The last 5% are those who will always be difficult to counsel, but managers report high satisfaction with this approach because it means that they win with the other 95%.

27. **A.** In spite of all the years that organizations have spent wrestling with this problem, the process of supervisory rating usually is invalid (and therefore legally indefensible). This doesn't mean that there aren't some approaches that are a whole lot better than the usual rating forms (e.g., criterion-based, critical incident, peer review, self-evaluation) and which are worth doing. But for the most part, managers report that they get little or no value out of the process which is still largely of the older school of subjective ratings.

28. **A.** Except for creating an historical document or building a case, there really is no common sense reason why performance appraisal should be focused on the past period of time. The primary purposes are to let people know where they stand now so that plans can be laid to take them from that point to the next level of performance, and to see what work objectives are related to their responsibilities. A manager can't control backward in time, only forward. Too often, appraisal systems have operated from a legalistic, documenting frame of reference, rather than from a frame of reference of how to build people and the business.

V. POSITIVE DISCIPLINE

29. **A.** From a practical standpoint, it doesn't make much sense to try to change all the annoying idiosyncracies people bring to work. Yet many managers get unduly irritated, perhaps due to their own stress and frustrations, over behaviors that aren't worth changing or which aren't central to the job. Effective managers overlook, tolerate, and forgive. If it would be useful to point out the problem to the employee, go ahead. However, if change doesn't take place, it's probably best to forget the problem unless analysis shows it to be costly.

30. **DA.** It's true that this is a corporate record being created by the supervisor to help communicate and control the problem internally, and to be used in later legal action, if necessary. But there's no reason not to inform the employee that the record is being created to serve as documentation. This communicates clearly that management is serious. It is not recommended that the employee be allowed to read the record.

31. **A.** If the message is only negative, the employee will think he's being written off. It's been found that framing the bad news within the picture of the employee's positive behavior is more likely to lead to a change away from the negative behavior. The employee clearly sees that he is generally held in regard, but that a limited area of performance is of concern.

32. **DA.** A common perception among management is that personnel executives take the side of employees and make it unnecessarily difficult to discipline or terminate employees. What they are encountering is not a resistance on the part of the personnel professional, but rather legal or policy requirements as to how such problems must be handled. Personnel management will nearly always help the manager get a problem person out of the organization, but they must do it by the book.

33. **DA.** Punishment may turn the person around, but it may not. The problem with punishment approaches is that they are not predictable in terms of later employee behavior. That being so, it's usually best to try other approaches first. If they work, they won't carry with them the sting and negativism that sometimes is a residue of punishment.

34. **A.** An employee should be viewed as clearing his record if he maintains acceptable behavior standards for an acceptable time frame. There is no value in holding past misdeeds over a person's head, or continuing to label with names that no longer apply. However, it also makes sense to insist on an acceptably long period of time for this to occur. Otherwise, managers report encountering the person who keeps his nose clean for six months, then recycles the old problems all over again. In other words, what constitutes clear evidence of changed behavior rather than temporary compliance is a key issue in rehabilitation.

35. **A.** Like every rule of thumb, it isn't hard and fast, and shouldn't be applied in all cases. However, if there have been repeated failures to comply with expected job and personal standards, it is increasingly probable that management will not be successful with this person. It's doubtful that forty chances at improvement should be given, and one chance probably isn't enough. For the good of the organization it's usually best not to draw things out too long.

VI. SPECIAL CASES

36. **A.** These are the most common manifestations of mental disturbance or illness. The supervisor does not need to be able to label people, or understand all the dynamics at play, but he does need to know when he's facing something more than an employee who's just temporarily upset. At that point, the supervisor's important function is to get such an employee referred to a professional.

37. **A.** It's easier to deal with job performance problems because of the supervisor's knowledge of the job and existing job standards, and because job performance problems can be judged by behavioral observation. Personal problems are often psychological, involve outside factors of which the supervisor is unaware, and require a set of counseling and interpersonal skills that may be beyond the supervisor's skills. To be successful at handling these personal problems requires the manager to be as knowledgeable as possible of the employee's background, personality, and motivation patterns.

38. **DA.** These four factors are the best tools to use in attendance control: defined rules, consistent penalties, accurate records, and singling out excessive and high frequency violators. An absentee control program using these four factors has a much higher chance of success than other approaches.

39. **DA.** This is a common misconception. While alcoholics will usually have a higher lost time record, those absences will be scattered through the work week. Often these absences are partial days, with reason found to leave the work place early (as opposed to latecoming).

40. **A.** Employees who are chemically dependent are in the grip of a powerful force which usually disables them from responding to counseling or less severe approaches. The threat of job loss is often the only force powerful enough to drive them into counseling. A common report from spouses is that the supervisor was able to get the employees into a rehabilitation program after all of their own efforts had failed.

41. **A.** Knowing that their skills are impaired by drug use, along with a lower achievement drive caused by the drug, many users deliberately look for jobs that are beneath their capabilities. From their viewpoint, this allows them to continue to function in a job which makes less demand on them, and the resulting economic security allows them to feed their habit.

42. **A.** Not all accident victims are emotionally or mentally disturbed, but a high percentage of them are. People with job accident histories are likely to repeat. This behavior is a form of self-punishment, and allows them to economically survive off their employer without having to work. This behavior has been termed a mental illness by experts in the field.

VII. DISCIPLINARY PROCEDURES

43. **A.** While only a few employees require control via written policy, these few justify the existence of the policy. It has been said that the bottom line in managing problem employees is that they have to know there is a bottom line! Like sign posts on the road, the policy that is necessary primarily for the few does serve to let all others know what the boundaries and rules for the road are.

44. **DA.** A rulebook written to cover all situations would be bigger than the Encyclopedia Britannica. Too many things to remember means that nothing gets remembered. In practice, it's been found that a few enforced rules are more helpful to the organization and the employee than a lot of rules that are ignored.

45. **DA.** While a rule may not have been enforced in the past because it was not needed, it remains alive as long as the organization intends to apply it against violators. However, the rule for all intents and purposes is dead if it is not used in situations that call for it. When a rule has become dead, but management intends to start enforcing it in the future, it's usually best to communicate that the rule is being resurrected, and will be used in the future.

46. **DA.** Effective formal disciplinary procedures in the past often established elaborate multi-level, multi-channel approaches that tied up the organization and the employee in a quasi-legal system. More contemporary approaches usually keep the steps to a minimal number and operate as simple a system as possible, still allowing for a stepwise, due process review. In the case of severe violations, some systems call for no warnings at all beyond initial employee orientation. In every case, the enforcement of discipline must comply with whatever corporate approach is being followed.

47. **A.** A performance contract removes a lot of ambiguity over what the expectations are. Once the employee signs such a work plan, there is clear evidence that communications on these items took place, and that the employee agreed to the conditions set forth. A lot of waffling behavior tends to go away when things get nailed down in this fashion.

48. **DA.** As a general rule, the penalty severity should be in relation to the employee's performance in relation to the specific rule violated. The violation of other rules should not influence the penalty given. However, if the organization policy specifically allows for a cumulative approach to discipline, where several rule violations allow for a harsher penalty, and this is known by employees, then the harsher penalty is allowable.

49. **DA.** Discipline is a positive part of the supervisor's job. To make people disciples is to make them followers of the good and true path. This followership is most pleasantly obtained through training, communication and counseling, and teaching by example. But if harsher approaches are required, the end goal is still a positive one: helping people successfully fulfill correct standards of performance.

VIII. EMPLOYEE TERMINATION

50. **DA.** Managers often use this line of thinking to justify not facing the difficulty of a termination. The truth is that they are perpetuating a situation that keeps the failing employee a loser. They are destroying the employee's home life, sense of personal esteem and self respect, and preventing him/her from moving on to a better life adjustment elsewhere. A more inhumane and uncaring supervisory attitude can hardly be imagined.

51. **A.** While few people enjoy being fired, it does cause them to re-evaluate what they are doing with their lives, and to move on into a new phase of existence. The evidence is that most people gain in this process. One year after termination, about 80% of those terminated report that it "was the best thing that could have happened to me".

52. **A.** There comes a point at which management has done all it can to help the person turn around. Beyond that point there should be no delay to separate people who do not enjoy either doing good work or relating to other members of the team. To delay at this stage will sap group morale, perpetuate tensions, and erode standards.

53. **DA.** To delay suspension or termination allows the poor performer to stir up other employees or to commit some act of retribution. Those who are about to be severely disciplined know that it's coming. Once the decision to act has been made, move immediately.

54. **A.** This general principle in the law is known as Employment at Will. The employee is employed at the will of the employer, and the employer can decide to no longer employ for nearly any reason. The major exceptions to this principle are employment/union contracts, and such criteria as are specified in the case law (discrimination cases). This doctrine has been eroded by court decisions in recent years when the courts have become concerned about "unjust firings" and other badly handled approaches that employers have used. Nonetheless, as a general rule, Employment at Will still means that employers should feel comfortable in insisting that employees meet standards of performance and conduct, and that they can remove employees who do not.

55. **A.** This is particularly true when the violation is severe, such as stealing, causing physical harm, or gross insubordination. While in any given case, the court might uphold Employment at Will (see the above answer) without documentation or due process, for less severe violations the provision of evidence and due process is still a likely requirement.

56. **A.** It's rare to have a perfect case in a court appearance. Both a complaining employee and the organization will have defects in their arguments. The courts will generally look for evidence of fairness, objectivity, and consistency on the part of the employer. In considering how firm the ground is for dealing with a particular case, a manager might want to consider whether those three variables are present.

Action Plan
for
Problem Employee
Managing

Dr. V. Clayton Sherman

INSTRUCTIONS

Following are a number of actions that might be taken in handling a problem employee. Complete an Action Plan for **each** problem case you are working on. To get a picture of what you've done with the employee up to this point, first place a mark next to the items in the DONE column for actions already taken.

Now go back through the list of suggested actions and place a mark next to those items that need to be done in the **NEED TO DO** column. (You can later place a mark in the **DONE** column when these actions are completed).

Finally, complete the Summary of Needed Actions at the end of the Action Plan. This will allow you to sequence next steps and set a calendar of events

---

EMPLOYEE

MANAGER   **DATE COMPLETED**

Additional copies are available. For information, write to Dr. V. Clayton Sherman, c/o AMACOM Books. 135 W. 50th St.. New York, NY 10020.

INITIAL CASE ASSESSMENT

NEED TO DO   DONE

☐ ☐   1. Describe the problem specifically and behaviorally: What should they start/stop doing?

☐ ☐   2. Gather data to verify problem specifics and range.

☐ ☐   3. Calculate costs and impacts of problem employee's behavior. Is it important enough to really warrant further management action?

☐ ☐   4. Talk with the employee to get his/her side of things in discussion that is primarily fact gathering.

☐ ☐   5. Decide: Is this a problem employee, or simply an employee with a problem? Is he/she the problem, or is he/she merely problemed?

☐ ☐   6. Other: _____

_____

_____

ORIENTATION AND TRAINING

NEED TO DO   DONE

☐ ☐   7. Decide: Does the person have the intelligence and capability to do the job? If not, transfer the employee to another job, redesign the present job, or terminate.

☐ ☐   8. Should employee recycle through initial orientation and job training? Don't rely on education if this is primarily an attitude or personality problem.

☐ ☐   9. If employee has the intelligence and aptitude, but hasn't used skills lately, provide more practice on the job, perhaps as part of a buddy system.

☐ ☐   10. Provide training in new skills if job has changed.

☐ ☐   11. Other: _____

_____

_____

COUNSELING AND COMMUNICATIONS

NEED TO DO   DONE

☐ ☐   12. Add to documentation: record factual information and all steps taken. Keep the record clean of unsupported opinions and judgments. Review employee record to see if earlier documents support current picture.

☐ ☐   13. Decide: Do you really want to retrieve the employee or just be rid of him/her? Are you connected enough to the employee to be able to help?

☐ ☐   14. Provide "word to the wise" counseling: a short verbal feedback session to review facts, expression of displeasure, and confidence that employee will correct the problem.

☐ ☐   15. Conduct a formal performance appraisal session. Be clear in your mind as to what you're trying to achieve.

☐ ☐   16. Set up a written and signed performance contract with the employee, complete with objectives, specific action plans where applicable, standards of performance, and dates of review and completion.

☐ ☐   17. Decide: Is there a personality conflict which makes it impossible for you to connect with this person? Transfer may be the best solution, but don't do it if there is no reason to believe that things will be better with another boss.

☐ ☐   18. Engage in power counseling, the "shape up or ship out" talk. Use this technique only if you have high self confidence and believe in salvageability of the employee. Since this technique includes a final warning, review the Termination Procedures below before conducting the session so you'll be prepared in the event employee does not respond.

☐ ☐   19. Other: _____

_____

_____

REFERRAL ACTIONS

NEED TO DO   DONE

☐ ☐   20. Stop further counseling effort, and either take more direct actions or refer employee when: 1) two sessions have produced little or no change in an employee who seems upset or emotionally disturbed; 2) three or four sessions have produced no result in an employee who seems emotionally stable.

☐ ☐   21. Refer employee to Personnel or Employee Assistance Plan Administrator.

☐ ☐   22. Refer employee for professional help (physician, psychologist, treatment center).

☐ ☐   23. Refer employee to another member of line management, usually higher in the hierarchy.

☐ ☐   24. Other: _____

_____

_____

MANAGE THE REWARD SYSTEM

NEED TO DO DONE

25. Remove organizational and environmental obstacles to proper performance (e.g., lack of resources or management support, insufficient time, poor organization climate, etc.).

26. Remove any existing punishments that may be preventing positive behavior (e.g., poor group norms, new salary less than previous hourly wage plus overtime for same work).

27. Eliminate any existing recognition, reinforcement or rewards for bad behavior (e.g., pay for lost time, recognizing employees only when they misbehave).

28. Provide additional recognition, reinforcement, or rewards for good behavior (e.g., "attaboys", incentives, special rewards for specific behaviors).

29. Reduce employee's salary in present job, cut performance bonus, reduce job grade, or give a suspension (with or without pay).

30. Other: _____

JOB DESIGN AND RESTRUCTURING

NEED TO DO DONE

31. Redesign employee's current job to elevate or lower content to meet employee's capabilities. Is he/she capable of doing any job if not the present one?

32. Transfer the employee to another job or unit. Don't do this if it's just going to pass along the problem to another supervisor. Transfer is appropriate if it corrects a case of "square peg in a round hole".

33. Demote the employee. Usually this is based on an in-house job regrading procedure, and is appropriate where competence and good attitude are present.

34. Other: _____

DISCIPLINARY PROCEDURES

NEED TO DO DONE

35. Activate the organization's disciplinary or warning system. Follow the in-house policy to communicate what's expected, what's wrong in current performance, how employee should improve, when, and consequences of failure to do so.

36. Issue appropriate followup warnings (verbal or written) if following a step system.

37. Allow employee sufficient opportunity to improve by giving time, means, and support.

38. Place employee on probation for a set period of time. Any further violation during the probation period would usually result in termination.

39. Place employee on suspension with pay to give management time to review the facts. Suspension without pay is usually reserved as a course of punishment.

40. Gross acts of misconduct, whether of commission or omission, call for no stepwise progression. Go to termination procedures.

41. Other: _____

TERMINATION PROCEDURES

NEED TO DO DONE

42. Review entire situation with personnel department or legal counsel. The review may not lead to termination, but is particularly appropriate when the manager has done everything he/she can think of and needs a "sort it out" session.

43. Review situation with chain of command executive.

44. Issue final warning. This is not necessary in all cases.

45. Decide: Do the circumstances suggest supportive outplacement services (e.g., job placement assistance) or more than minimum separation payments and allowances?

46. Offer employee option of voluntary resignation.

47. Terminate the employee.

48. Anticipate and plan for work group anxiety and response. Will any "damage control" be necessary?

49. Review what went wrong to avoid this problem next time.

50. Other: _____

SUMMARY OF NEEDED ACTIONS

Now that you've selected a number of **NEED TO DO** actions, enter these in the following action plan in the sequence that makes most sense for your situation.

Action #	Specific Action Needed	Operational Notes	Date Begin	Date Complete

4

Eight Steps to Positive Prevention

In this portion of our discussion, we'll focus on an eight-step process for the positive prevention of problem employees, an overview of which is presented in Figure 1. In Chapter 7, you'll see a second eight-step process, that one for the positive discipline of problem employees.

An ounce of prevention *is* worth a pound of cure, and managerial experience certainly bears out the fact that creating conditions that prevent the development of problem employees is a lot smarter course of action than trying to deal with problem employees later on. If we fail to do those things that keep people on the straight and narrow, let employees get off track, and then try to correct the situation, it's just a lot more work than it needed to be. Admittedly, it's a lot of work to get people into the grooves of proper performance, but if we don't get them into those grooves, and if we're not careful about finding ways to put up protective barriers that will keep people functioning correctly, then we're going to have to do another type of work, and that other work is less pleasant, takes longer, is more emotional, and is politically more risky to our careers. And that other work is the work of dealing with people once they've gone off track. So my earnest invitation is for you to pay careful attention to what we're about to discuss, because if you've got some problem people now, this eight-step approach will help you prevent more of them.

1. Select Good People

The first step in the eight-step process for positive prevention is to exercise care in your initial selection process. It's possible to hire good people, just as it's possible to hire people who are an accident in search of someplace to happen.

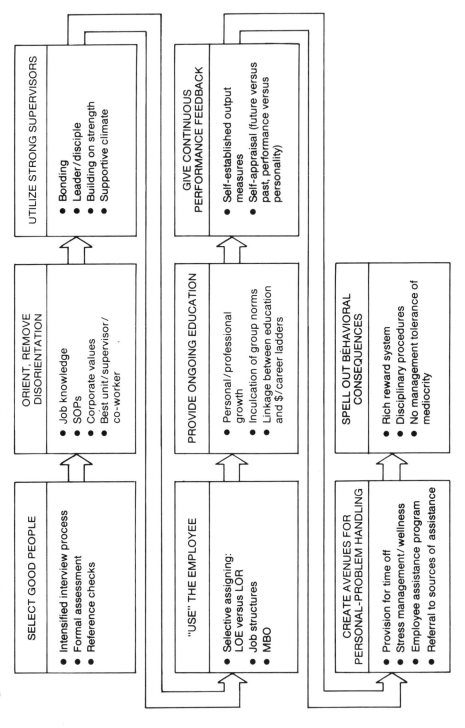

Figure 1. Positive prevention of problem employees.

In some instances, because of the sloppy selection methods used in the past, you may now be living with a problem person, perhaps selected by your predecessor, and the individual in question has been a problem from day one. He came to your organization with a set of inappropriate attitudes and a set of inadequate skills, and now you're living with the effects. If a better job of selection had been done, it might have been possible to select out, avoid hiring, someone like this. So I would suggest that a lot of time and attention be given to the selection process. One way in which that can be done is simply to institute a more intensive interviewing process.

The interview remains the primary means of selection by which most people are hired into most organizations. If you examine the process used in your own organization, what you may typically find is that one or two people do most of the hiring for your department or division. Furthermore, you're likely to find that the amount of time spent in that hiring process is relatively short. By that I mean not more than two hours, and usually less than an hour for nontechnical people. While this is not a book on personnel selection, here are some simple rules of thumb, practical guidelines for how one might intensify the selection process.

Longer interviews. Simply interview for longer periods of time than you now do. If you now interview for 30 minutes, interview for an hour. If you now interview for an hour, interview for two. The likelihood that candidates will say something stupid or totally inappropriate, or say something that gives you a better insight into the way their mind really works, is going to be greater the longer you are exposed to them.

Multiple interviewers. Have more than one person do the interviewing. Multiple interviewers will increase the range of questions and the range of perspectives that a job candidate has to deal with in the course of discussing his or her future with your organization. Bill may find out some things about this individual that Harry didn't, and Harry will learn some things that Ruth didn't. And as the three of them swap information together after the interview sessions, they will reach a far more accurate decision than if any one of them had had to do the job alone. That's a known principle from decision making: "Two (or more) brains are better than one."

Multiple interviews. The third simple rule is to have your prospects come back for multiple interviews. An interview is the world's phoniest situation. Candidates show up in their best clothes. They are on their best behavior, displaying their best manners. You'll never see them looking that good or acting that courteous again! If the first impression was positive, then have them back for a second interview. If the second impression is also strongly positive, you may in fact have a winner.

It's been reported that at a well-known New York nightclub, a busboy candidate has to go through five one-hour interviews! One of the advantages of that process is that it gives you multiple impressions of the person over time. Sometimes there are things we can't quite put our finger on in the first interview, but as we get acquainted, while the interviewee is not yet on our payroll, we come to either like or dislike the person. Yes, it may be inconvenient for the candidate, but it will certainly measure his degree of motivation or interest in your job, and it will save you from the disaster of hiring somebody completely inappropriate.

Inconvenience interview. At least one of the interview sessions ought to be very early on a Monday morning. People who are substance abusers tend to binge on weekends, and it's possible that at 7 o'clock on Monday morning, you'll see some of the symptoms of their chemical dependency: nervousness, popping breath mints, blood-shot eyes, clammy skin, and so forth.

Tardiness knockout. A somewhat controversial principle of selection interviewing, but one that I believe the evidence supports, is that if candidates come late to the interview, don't hire them. Now it's possible they have a good excuse for why they're late. Except in very rare circumstances (say, a flash flood that paralyzes transportation systems), don't hire them. It's true that if you follow the rule of not hiring latecomers, you might be ruling out good people, but the probabilities are against it.

It is in the interview stage when people are trying to make their best impression; that's when they're most motivated to measure up in your eyes. They want this job. If with all of that motivation going for them, they still can't manage to come to the interview on time, are you willing to bet they're going to come to work on time once they're on the payroll? The evidence indicates otherwise.

Interview training. Putting all the managers in your organization through a training seminar on interviewing makes a lot of sense. In the seminars that we conduct, we see managers learning new and better selection techniques. The process of full discussion and sharing experience helps to sharpen their approaches, and it helps the organization change those practices that really have not been effective.

Formal assessment. Other organizations go even further and engage in formal assessment methods, such as assessment centers, psychological testing, and depth or stress interviewing. With these approaches, an outside service is generally retained to assess people on various characteristics — intelligence, aptitude, personality, interests, values, and the like. In a typical testing process, the candidate would take eight hours of tests and answer about 4,000 questions. Those test-response patterns can be grouped and matched to validated profiles of what it takes to be successful in certain jobs. The output to management is a five- to seven-page report, along with a sheet profiling all the test scores. While that kind of technique doesn't do your selection for you, it does provide an additional screening tool that you can use to supplement your own interviewing efforts.

My suggestion to clients who are interested in these more advanced procedures is to try them once with a particular candidate. Try them as an experiment to see what additional information is revealed that would not have been determined in the normal selection process. A second way to test out whether these assessment measures are really any good is to go through the process yourself and see what the selection report is on you! A lot of executives who have tried that experiment find it scary that they can be sized up so accurately.

Reference checking. The reference-checking process has become virtually worthless in America as more and more organizations are reluctant to give honest information for fear of litigation. Nonetheless, I would certainly recommend that you check references. There are some skillful ways in which one can get at least some basic information. The previous employer may tell you that your prospect is absolutely wonderful, terrific, walks on water, and wouldn't harm a fly. To determine the validity of that good news, ask the test question, "Is this person eligible for rehire?" If the answer is no, this suggests that there is some discrepancy between the previous employer's words and the reality of the employee's performance. On the other hand, it's possible that former employee may not be eligible for rehire because the organization has an internal policy that prohibits it. In other words, the employee may truly be a good person who is simply ineligible for rehire.

If you get a no on the rehire question, you must then ask the next question, "Does your company have a policy that prohibits rehiring people?" If the previous employer says no, then the chances are good that there's been a problem with this person and that the reference isn't leveling with you. Some organizations go beyond their own personal reference checking and use various credit report services, which can dig out additional evidence.

The point I'm making is that the best way to prevent having to deal with problem employees later on is to try to select people with good attitudes and adequate skills up front. If you do that, you'll save a lot of headaches down the road.

2. Orient, Remove Disorientation

Orientation as it's practiced in most organizations is a joke. A person comes on board, gets a half-morning session with the personnel people, who show him how to fill out the insurance forms and where the disaster escape routes are, and is then sent back to the unit. There we have a typically lightweight approach to orienting new employees to their job and the organization. See if your firm measures up. Does it follow the guidelines presented in this section?

One way to view the orientation needs of employees is to keep in mind that they are 100 percent *disoriented* when they walk in the door. They don't know you, they don't know the people, they don't know the procedures, they don't know the work, they don't know the customers, they don't know where to hang their hat, they don't know where the rest room is. Management's decision is truly not one of whether there should be an investment in orientation but whether it wants to allow totally disoriented people to function within the organization.

In many companies, management has chosen to force people to learn the ropes by themselves in a trial-and-error process. In the course of making errors and by going through trials, these bumping-into-walls employees create problems, injure their self-image, get undeserved reputations, and almost immediately start to drift off track. The reason they're off track is that they were never put on track. They were not told where the track is, when the train leaves, or where they're supposed to get off. It's not fair, it's not honest, it doesn't make any sense at all for a manager to leave an employee in that state.

Far from resenting initial guidance, the best of your new hires will be quite receptive to it. Managers who neglect or postpone orientation may find themselves with a potentially effective employee who is starting to flounder, as in the following example:

Manager: Sally, I've been reviewing your performance records, and I'm a little puzzled. Things don't seem to be in line with the quantity and quality that I normally expect from professionals. Tell me, how do you think things are going?

New Employee:	Generally okay. I do as much work, and work as hard, as anybody else.
Manager:	Sally, you're still fairly new here, and I wanted you to understand exactly what I expect from you. I think that you should be aware that your performance volume compared to other new people is a little low, and the quality of your writing leaves something to be desired. I know you're working hard, and I believe that this is definitely not an attitude or motivation problem. I'm very pleased with you as a person, but I think I need to work with you on report writing and meeting deadlines. Would you mind letting me make some suggestions?
New Employee:	Not at all! I'd welcome the help . . .

At Sony, new employees go through 8 weeks of initial orientation, at IBM 16. General Motors' new Saturn plant provides for substantial employee involvement and intensive orientation, even though most of the new hires are former UAW employees from other locations. The trend and pattern in American industry is now moving toward extremely intensive orientation.

Cover All the Basics

What should the orientation include? Obviously, the mechanical housekeeping tasks necessary for personal support in the organization—how an employee gets a pay check, fills out the benefits forms, and those kinds of things—ought to be covered. A second knowledge area is in-depth training in terms of what the corporate values are. Employees like to know something about the history of the organization, why this organization is important, the kinds of customers served, what the products are, and what kind of contribution is being made to society.

What about the founder? What did he or she struggle with in order to make the organization possible? The history of the firm is extremely important because history is a series of stories, and stories convey the culture and values.

Some time ago, McDonald's first hamburger stand in Chicago was about to be closed. The traffic pattern in the area was no longer as good as it once had been, and McDonald's announced it would be tearing the building down. There came a flood of calls and letters from all across the United States informing management that it had its head in the sand because it did not appreciate the firm's own history. The fact is that McDonald's has become part of American culture and American history, and yet its management at first failed to see the value of the enterprise's own history.

It's amazing how often managements do not understand their company's own importance and hence do not convey that importance to their employees. What is it new employees want to feel? I think it's important that they see themselves as being part of an organization that's going somewhere, that has a noble purpose, and that has values. It's important that they regard the work they do for the firm as meaningful. But if nobody ever explains that to new hires, I don't know how they're supposed to magically generate this profound understanding on their own.

A third major area that new employees would like to know about is the specifics of their job. What are the tasks they're supposed to do, how fast are these tasks supposed to be done, what is the normal interaction between this unit and other units or between their job and other jobs that depend on it?

Particularly germane to our discussion of how we prevent employees from becoming problem people is that employees need to know what the performance standards are. How well do they have to do this job? What does it take to please the boss? What do they have to do in order to get a salary increase? What must they do in order to get a compliment? In some organizations, this information is treated like a big secret. In some organizations, managers couldn't answer those questions because they don't know themselves! But the best organizations are those that sit down very early with new employees and explain to them exactly what it takes so there isn't any mystery.

When employees know precisely what they have to do in order to get ahead in your organization, they'll aim for those targets. If you tell them what the objective of the game is, they'll pursue the objective. People are game players — that's not a bad label — and to win in the game called work, just tell them what the rules are! The work game is a lot like Monopoly. If you don't explain the rules, if you don't tell the players what it takes to pass Go, if you don't tell them what it takes to dominate that board and win by the rules, then they're going to go off on their own and play the game by other rules. So why don't we spell out exactly what it takes to succeed in this system?

If you're going to do this job well, it will take a substantial infusion of time and resources. I don't think this kind of thing can be accomplished in a morning or even a day or two. How much time it will take for your particular situation I don't know. Increasingly, we see organizations devoting days, weeks, and even months to the orientation process. These organizations want people to firmly understand, early in their employment life, what is expected and how to do what they've been paid to do. To the extent that your organization matches that profile and seems to match that intensity, you're probably doing well.

Organizations that fail to orient intensively run a very serious risk of having disoriented employees who, in turn, wind up disorienting the entire firm. What do I mean by that statement? In a very mobile society, fairly high turnover within organizations is becoming the norm. That factor, plus rapid change and growth within an organization, results in substantial percentages of people who have less than two or three years of service. As the mass of disoriented workers multiplies within an organization, they become the majority, and that can change the culture and alter the general way things are done around the firm. Our concern over orientation should involve not only setting new hires on the correct path but preserving the oganization itself. We simply have to defend against this massive amount of ignorance that walks in the door.

Place People Correctly

One very helpful technique in the orientation process is to ask where would be the best place to orient this individual and who would be the best person to do the job. If your organization is like most, there are some departments and some managers that you wish had less influence than they now have, and there are others that you wish you could clone so the rest of the organization would be like them. The basic rule is: If you have a choice, *assign new employees to the best units, best supervisors, and best co-workers.*

Within the organization, there are probably some high-performance units. If you can, send new employees to one of those units for at least a brief rotation period. Additionally, assign them to the best supervisor, that man or woman who is the task master (the master of the task), who has very high performance expectations, who seems to have a knack for getting people excited and turned on to their job responsibilities. Employees assigned to such a leader are more likely to get in the groove of understanding what they should do than employees assigned to a mediocre manager. In like fashion, if you team each new hire up with the best worker within that department in a buddy system, that buddy, with his or her very positive attitude and good performance history, will be a better teacher than almost anyone else in the unit. On the other hand, if you team new people up with just any bozo, don't be surprised if things turn into a circus. So let's consider what can be done in the original stages of employee connection to get people on the right track.

3. Utilize Strong Supervisors

Winners make winners, and losers make losers. Why is it that one of the best ways to prevent problem behavior is to assign employees to strong supervisors? Research has determined that strong supervisors act as a linchpin, tying their people to the rest of the organization. Problem supervisors, on the other hand, do not form a positive link with their people, and their employees are disconnected from the values, practices, and spirit of the rest of the firm. A classic *Harvard Business Review* article entitled "Pygmalion in Management" reported the finding that supervisors tend to have high expectations or low expectations and that employees, in turn, tend to perform at those levels.[1]

Imagine what would happen to a new employee who encountered a weak supervisor, one who did not strongly support the organization's values and who had low expectations for that employee's performance. There is a higher probability that a new hire assigned to that unit will be a problem in the future—that is, weak supervisors create problem employee behaviors through their lack of leadership and direction. It is therefore imperative that new employees not be assigned to such people within the first 12 months of their career.

John Hancock Mutual Life Insurance Company makes a practice of assigning new sales reps to the strongest managers in the field, thereafter rotating them to people who may be less strong. What the firm determined was that once employees had been put in a high-performance groove, they did not lessen their own performance when they encountered weaker supervisors later in their career. In fact, these properly trained new reps even wondered whether their second supervisors knew how things were supposed to be done!

The role modeling the supervisor does for new employees helps change behavior and teaches them how to behave. Good supervisory bonding is more likely to occur if the supervisor spends considerable time with new hires and is reassuring, helpful, and supportive. It is less likely to occur if the supervisor is distant, preoccupied, and harsh in his or her communications.

One of the key characteristics of good supervisors is their understanding that they have to lead their disciples. A disciple is a follower, and if employees are to be followers, they must see some leadership in the unit. Unfortunately, a lot of supervisors are only figureheads. Where there is no excellence in leadership, it is unlikely there will be any excellence in followership.

One of the test questions for any organization is just how good are its supervisors? And if the basic talent and aptitude are there, have supervisors been exposed to the concepts of role modeling and bonding? In your own supervisory behaviors, do you make it a point to get acquainted, to really know each subordinate? One of the comments one hears from inexperienced supervisors is that they feel they shouldn't be involved in their employees' personal lives, that they feel uncomfortable or out of line in doing so. While this may seem logical, it is usually not the most effective approach. The best managers know their employees; they often know their families, have been in their homes, or have had the employees in theirs. Because of this closeness, effective managers feel free to speak up and to make quick, correcting comments that warn employees when there's a difficulty at work. One almost gets the feeling of being in a family when working in such a unit. Have you linked the employees in your unit to you? Have you linked them to the organization by virtue of your behavior?

4. "Use" the Employee

Where did we ever get the idea that we shouldn't "use" people? How did the phrase "using people" acquire a negative connotation? I guess it smacks of manipulation. Well, I suggest that one of the biggest reasons why people become problems is because organizations haven't used them.

I remember the story a good friend of mine told me about how he had come to work for a major company with a recently acquired M.B.A. from Indiana University, one of the top business schools in the United States. The first task to which this young eager beaver was assigned was to clean out the storage case where all the old records and forms were kept! Said he, "The first message my management gave me was that I was only good for janitorial work."

I, too, vividly remember the very first assignment I was given when I got out of college. I thought I was pretty terrific, that I was going to set all kinds of performance records. My first assignment was to redesign a $3'' \times 5''$ card that was used to sign employees up for the firm's insurance coverage. I thought to myself: "Well, this certainly isn't very taxing of my vast talents. Nevertheless, I'll do it with great gusto." So I sat down at my desk and 60 minutes later produced for my boss's review said sign-up card. He indicated that it looked okay to him. He would take it "down the hall" to the departmental manager's meeting the following week.

To make a long story short, he took that card and its many revisions down the hall for the better part of six months! With each turndown, my initial confidence, my initial self-image, became more shaky. Is it possible that even I, with my profound insights, lacked the intelligence to design a 3″ × 5″ card? Before this particular project ended, the company had had me spend weeks of my life in forms-design seminars. I burned up the long-distance wires with forms consultants, I amassed the world's largest library of books on forms design, and still I couldn't satisfy those nit-picking perfectionists.

My mother used to say that the only reason I stayed in school longer than some of the other kids was because I was dumber! This project was beginning to make me think she was right! It took me six months to figure out that perhaps the problem lay not with the form but with something else in the organization. To test that theory, I resurrected the original design I had created six months earlier and sent it down the hall, only to have it approved! How was I used? How are we using people? Particularly, how are we using them in the early days of their career?

LOE Versus LOR

An old theory of motivation pointed out that people come to the job having a certain level of expectations. They anticipate finding certain things. These expectations are not necessarily realistic, but nonetheless, they are evident in people's thinking. They wish for a certain relationship with their boss, they anticipate certain group dynamics, they hope the job will be that great pinnacle of joy they've been looking for. But this level of expectation (LOE) encounters a second phenomenon called the level of reality (LOR). And the level of reality is often less than the level of expectation.

Suppose we give people with a high LOE a low LOR — namely, a job that is beneath their capabilities. Knowing their own capabilities, they now encounter a level of reality that is substantially lower, meaning they will be used at levels beneath their potential. That creates a dissonance, a disagreeable feeling. It creates frustration, anger, resentment.

On the other hand, a person might enter a job hoping to be able to do fairly well, and the LOR might generally be a pretty good match with what the new worker had expected. If the new job is perhaps slightly beyond his or her present capabilities, slightly more challenging, slightly more demanding, there is an energy created here, too. But the feeling in this case has positive overtones. It seems to be saying that the boss expects more of me, the boss thinks I can be more than I have been before. The job is really making me grow and stretch.

What's been found is that employees are more than willing to do the occasional scut-work job. Everybody, I think, is mature enough to understand that there is going to be some routine work that must be done. There's always some unpleasant task nobody likes to do. But the real question is, what is the pattern — and how does the level of reality compare with the level of expectation? If we're continually assigning people to a level of reality that is below their self-perception, their self-image, their own internally perceived LOE, it is going to create a lot of negative vibes. These people are going to be very angry and over a period of time will become uncooperative. We are sowing the seeds of new problem employee behaviors.

Use People Through Selective Assigning

Good supervisors have always understood the principle of selective assigning. You've got to figure out what would be a good stretching experience and throw in a few plums for every person in the unit occasionally. Jobs that are incessantly routine or mundane ought to be either redesigned, automated, computerized, or given to people with very little ability. There's no such thing as unworthy work, but it's a question of what we're asking people to do continually and what is the best way to use them.

My suggestion is to *use* the capabilities of the people around you — not so that people will feel used in the negative sense but so they will feel useful (that is, experience a fullness of use). Yet when I ask management audiences what percentage of their people are being utilized at 80, 90, or even 100 percent of their capacity, I get estimates that only 10 percent or 20 percent of the people are being fully challenged. What this means is that we are systematically not using people, we are systematically not freeing them up to do what should be done. We are putting people — not just a few people, but millions of people — into jobs and job structures that are less than the persons themselves. This creates a dehumanizing effect, it creates resentment, it creates the spectacle of people racing out the door at the end of the shift.

Job Structures and Career Management

Another aspect of employee utilization is to examine the adequacy of job structures. If an organization has large departments, sometimes natural career ladders will emerge, giving people a chance to move from one job to another. If we can't be flexible in the content of every job, can we be flexible in giving people the opportunity to move from job to job?

In addition to career ladders, are job-posting systems in place? Such systems basically give employees an opportunity to walk through the door into another job. It gives them a chance to make their wishes known, a sense of control over what they're doing, and a feeling of freedom within the workplace.

One of the reasons that a free-enterprise economy does so well is that it represents a free labor market and people can choose to move to new jobs. How would you like to work in Poland or China where the state assigns jobs, and an individual cannot change employers? That kind of bureaucratic thinking has condemned many people to work in jobs for which they may have neither talent, interest, nor liking.

It has always intrigued me to see the dichotomy in managers who believe in personal freedom when it comes to running the country but who can't see the value of personal freedom at work. When we create freedom at work, it means that employees can take some responsibility for their lives and move themselves into a better job fit — where the LOE and the LOR are going to be closer. I don't think it's fair to assume that the supervisor should be capable of placing every person and should know each one so well that somehow the supervisor assumes the entire burden in making all these decisions. What can he do that will put these decisions into the hands of people who have to do the work?

Planned Performance

In addition to the concepts of using people, selective assigning, and setting up more creative job structures, I would add one other approach under the heading of people utilization: the concept of managing by objectives. MBO has become less prevalent as a work system in the United States than it once was. I think that fact is directly correlated with the decline of American productivity. A lot of MBO systems did have some failings and problems, probably the biggest being that they became overgrown, ponderous, forms-heavy, and bureaucratic. MBO is basically a process by which a manager and his staff member sit down and decide what that staff member is going to do in the next 90 days. At the end of the 90 days, they examine what was done and how well it was done. The concept of planning for people's performance is particularly important when we're dealing with other supervisors who may work for us or with professional and technical people.

For our clients, we developed a planned-performance system that specifies what is to be done, project review and completion dates, the level of authority that the employee has to carry out a particular project, the priority of that project compared to others, and standards against which to measure results. All of this is reduced to some simple forms completed by the employee, and agreed to and modified by the supervisor. Then the performance contract (which is what those documents represent) governs what that person is going to be doing over the next 90 days above and beyond his or her normal duties. The point of all of this is that when we keep people on fairly short control periods like 90-day increments, it's much easier to spot when they start going off track. If we never set up any kind of a system, then we have no way of reviewing performance or determining when problems are occurring. This management system, which we've called MANSYS, will be discussed in Chapter 6 of this manual.

Lee Iacocca states that part of his success in the turnaround of Chrysler Corporation was his use of a quarterly, planned-performance approach. He reports that when he first started with Ford in marketing and sales, he noticed that the stockholders insisted on receiving a quarterly report of the company's progress. To those who owned the corporation, a quarterly earnings statement was important for monitoring how effectively management was doing its job. Iacocca reasoned that if it was good enough for the shareholders, it was good enough for him in terms of monitoring how well his people were doing.

Consider what is actually happening with a planned-performance approach. Employees gain both freedom and control over their boss by getting the boss to buy into a shortened, select agenda of tasks to be done. From the boss's point of view, he or she is getting his staff associate to buy into doing the tasks that the boss most wants to get done. The boss says to himself:

> I'm getting my troops to set some dates, I'm giving them what they're always saying they don't have enough of—the freedom to do it. I'm going to give them the authority levels they need. I'm going to give them the support, too; I'm not going to rain on their parade. But in 90 days, we're going to sit down and see where they are. And I'm going to hold them accountable for results.

All parties in this transaction gain what each respectively wants — the freedom and control that are *both* necessary if work is to be accomplished correctly.

Are your people given guidance under a planned-performance approach, or are they left to wander through the maze? Are priorities set for them that really establish what ought to be happening, or are they left to divine this through the organizational Ouija board? Employees who function under a planned-performance contract are less likely to get out of the groove and become problems. They're also most likely to have the fun and joy of successfully achieving their goals. And goal attainment becomes a self-reinforcing mechanism that keeps them wanting to achieve new goals.

5. Provide Ongoing Education

Every job tends, over time, to evolve in such a way that its demands exceed the current capability of the job holder. In every job, the knowledge base keeps shifting and expanding. In every job, there is a risk that the person will reach a level of incompetence. Nearly 20 years ago, a popular book, *The Peter Principle,* stated that people eventually become promoted to their level of incompetence. I strongly disagree with that concept, for if it were true, it would mean that the executives who make these promotion decisions would themselves have to be incompetent to select so many incompetents.

I believe what actually happens is that executives generally promote people who are competent. Though these people may have much to learn, and though they may have to scramble at first to master the new task, they are able to do so and perform their work acceptably. But whatever the job, the knowledge explosion hits these promoted individuals, and that, coupled with the rule that change is continuous, creates quicksand — a morass into which they sink. People are not promoted to their level of incompetence. Rather, they are promoted to their level of competence, but the ground then gives way beneath them.

However it comes about, people's skills have to be updated. If they're not updated, these people are going to become less and less capable, and we'll have the beginnings of still more problem employees. Therefore, the corporation has to assume a nurturing role in sponsoring opportunities that will provide for both personal and professional growth, even if it becomes necessary to mandate employee participation.

One of the smartest things that can be done is to create an atmosphere of professional growth and an education orientation within your organization. In times past, educators used to talk about career education or vocational training. The view of education was that it ended when you reached eighth grade (at least, that was the idea back in the early 1900s). Or it ended when you reached twelfth grade (at least, that was the view in the thirties). In the fifties, we thought it ended when you graduated with a bachelor's degree. And in the seventies, it ended when you got your master's. But what we're now beginning to understand is that education has to be regarded as a lifelong learning process.

Lifelong learning within the corporation has to be considered a major management responsibility. If we can get that kind of atmosphere strongly entrenched in the group norms and group culture, it will help people maintain high levels of contribution. McDonald's runs a series of programs through Hamburger University. As silly as that sounds, in a business that many might think of as very simple (all they're making is hamburgers and fries), there is a real understanding that lifelong learning and systematic professional growth are essential business functions. Any organization that is systematically trying to groom its people, and keeps grooming them year after year after year, is an organization that is sending strong signals to its workforce that staying sharp is important. It's important personally, professionally, and organizationally. The best of organizations know that such a massive undertaking prevents hundreds, even thousands, of problem employee behaviors. Whatever its up-front costs, they are minor compared to the costs that would otherwise be incurred.

Some organizations even go so far in sponsoring development and education that they tie both promotion and pay increases to educational attainment. To be considered for promotion to the next highest level or to be considered for a merit increase, the employee knows he will have to complete a certain number of hours or courses at an acceptable competency level. What happens when rewards are tied to development and education? You get virtually 100 percent compliance by employees as people scramble aboard the bandwagon.

If you don't insist and set standards for knowledge gain, what will you get? Recently I was invited into a major medical center to work with its managers in an ongoing series of programs. In fact, I was asked to conduct an entire management course. In the planning session with these good folks, they indicated that they expected their managers to have an attendance rate of 80 percent to 85 percent. I naturally inquired about the missing 15 percent to 20 percent and was told, "They don't really come to anything we ever offer." The planners saw this as, in effect, a voluntary program. When asked whether they wouldn't like the others to attend, as well — particularly in view of the ambitious scope and cost of the project — they conceded not only that they would prefer 100 percent attendance but that the holdouts were, in all likelihood, the ones most in need of training! I asked whether a mandatory-attendance policy had ever been considered — on the grounds that, as professionals on the same management team, everyone should take this opportunity to master the same set of concepts, the same terminology, the same values. One executive, acknowledging the considerable merit of that suggestion but nevertheless falling back on tradition, indicated that "We've never done it that way." Since a change in this area struck me as long overdue — especially given everyone's agreement on the importance both of the program's message and of upgrading employee performance — I bluntly asked what management was afraid of. In a nutshell: employee resistance — the wrath of those who "won't like it." "Well, then," I replied, "just who's really managing your organization?" My final question was greeted with total silence.

To their great credit, the planners ultimately decided that this was too important a task for the organization to just let it drift or let people do whatever they wanted. They made attendance mandatory.

How strong are the ongoing educational and professional opportunities, both in and out of the firm where you work? How good are they within your own department, in your own area of departmental responsibility? What could be done to upgrade them?

6. Give Continuous Performance Feedback

Another step toward the positive prevention of problem employees is to provide continuous performance feedback. Let people know where they stand, and let them know on a regular basis. People want to know how they're doing. Most organizations respond by letting them know once a year. Wonderful! How would you like to be a member of a bowling league and go bowling every week, maybe two or three times a week, but get your scores once a year? How would you like to follow your favorite baseball team all season long and never get a peek at the scoreboard except at the end of the season? How would you like to date somebody you were crazy about without a clue as to whether or not he or she likes you till twelve months from now? Does this cockamamie idea make any sense to you? When I talk to managers around the United States, it doesn't seem to make any sense to them either. And there's almost unanimous agreement that they hate performance appraisal the way it's presently done.

Chapters 5 and 6 will offer a detailed discussion of performance appraisal. At this point, let's simply state that managers who do not devise a system that allows employees to know how they're doing are managers who are setting their employees up to fail. There is real discomfort with this task on the part of most managers, and it's clear that we need a far better approach than the one managers find so uncomfortable.

Briefly stated, the systems that do work are self-appraisal, where the employee measures his or her own performance against established output measures, and quarterly work planning and review (the MBO approach). We also know that performance appraisal that seeks to measure where the person is now so that we can plan for the future is far better than an approach that only looks backward at whatever failings occurred over the last year. And finally, performance evaluation should assess performance, not personality factors.

If we have an effective system for telling people where they stand, we know that good people will try to correct their behavior. But if we don't provide that helpful information, how can they possibly correct, hope to understand, or even know what they're doing?

7. Create Avenues for Personal-Problem Handling

The seventh step in our eight-step approach to positive prevention is the provision of avenues for personal-problem handling. Every individual is going to have personal problems at some point in his or her life. There's going to be illness, death in the family, possibly a divorce — unhappiness of one sort or another. And how, within our work situation, are we prepared to handle those problems? If we do not provide avenues, employees will be left to their own devices — and good luck to the employer.

As an example of the dilemmas that inadequate management preparation can create when difficulty strikes, some organizations allow two weeks of sick leave a year, with no provision for extended leave or disability. That's nice if the employee's illness happens to fit neatly into a two-week period, but what are you going to do if it doesn't? Other organizations will say, "Well, we can't pay you for more than two weeks, but we'll allow you to take whatever time you need as personal time and keep your job open for you." That, at least, seems a more flexible and humane approach than saying that because you can't curtail your sickness period, you're out.

The question that I'm raising here is just how flexible are a firm's policies in letting people work out their own problems? Some organizations have really thought this through and have come up with full-blown employee assistance programs (EAPs). An increasing number of organizations are taking some of the older supportive functions such as the industrial health unit, benefits administration, and whoever handled light counseling duties in the personnel department and adding to those a whole range of other functions that are integrated and coordinated for greater impact. Some of the new services include professional psychiatric counseling, alcohol rehabilitation, drug-counseling programs, income tax assistance, day-care centers, stress-management training, wellness programs, physical fitness, diet counseling, and health-club memberships. The range of options is almost limitless.

Employees don't forget it when the organization stands by them. In fact, employee loyalty, a phrase that has been meaningless in American industry for the last 30 years, is being won back by those organizations insightful enough to provide meaningful, broad-based resources for employees in crisis or for those just needing some support. The corporation that has the reputation among its employees for being there in the clinches is an organization that not only keeps people who are starting to sink from going under but creates a much more positive sense of allegiance among all the others who right now are not troubled. They know they will be supported if they run into a jam. In the research I've done, this has also been found to have a positive return on investment in terms of subsequent savings in lowered medical costs, workers' compensation claims, and so on.

While these support programs and avenues don't necessarily solve the person's problems, they may help him or her get through that rough spot. Getting people through the rough spots, getting them back to a point of normalcy, is what it's all about. So just how adequate is our support system? Are there additional elements that might be put into place to serve as backstops or preventive mechanisms?

8. Spell Out Behavioral Consequences

The last step in the review of positive prevention is to examine the behavioral consequences that exist in the organization. Let's start with a simple declaration of behavioral principles that are common knowledge:

1. Behavior that is reinforced, rewarded, and recognized is likely to be repeated.
2. Behavior that is not reinforced, rewarded, or recognized is likely to extinguish, or diminish gradually.

The preceding principles apply to both good behavior and bad behavior: Good (or bad) behavior that is reinforced is likely to be repeated, just as good (or bad) behavior that is not reinforced is likely to diminish gradually.

Given those principles, what is the reward system like in your organization? What is it that gets rewarded? I'd like you to think of some of the behaviors that a lot of organizations inappropriately reward. If you're sick and stay home from work, we pay you. If you have an accident and cause serious injury to yourself and considerable property damage, we pay you. If we lack the knowledge or courage to take action against you as a problem employee, we pay you each week for continuing your unsatisfactory performance. If you retire and leave the firm forever, we pay. If you die, we pay. So we have developed systems that reward all kinds of behaviors that don't really help the organization and that sometimes cause a repetition of unwanted behaviors. Again, behavior that is reinforced, rewarded, or recognized is going to be repeated.

And what happens to the person who has a perfect attendance record, the person who's never sick? As Red Buttons would say, "He never got a dinner!" What about the person who always supports the team? "He never got a dinner!" What about the person who offers more good ideas than anyone else? "She never got a dinner!" We don't recognize them at all. We lavish hours of our time and the bulk of our attention on the troublemaker, but the solid performer doesn't get the time of day.

The single most frequent comment that employees write on attitude surveys is this: "The only time you hear anything from management is when you do something wrong." Does this make any sense to you? Don't get me wrong: I'm not against sick leave or vacation pay or those kinds of benefits. I'm simply saying that we sometimes send a funny set of signals that are at variance with how people normally make the associations that guide behavior.

Are there some payments, recognitions, or rewards that could be provided for people who are perfect attenders or superior achievers? Of course. One organization has an "Academy Awards" banquet each year for people who have demonstrated the most notable accomplishments in a variety of categories. Another company picks an employee as "hero of the month." Yet another organization has a multifaceted recognition system that continues throughout the year. There are spur-of-the-moment certificates, distribution of S&H Green Stamps, printed brownie points and atta-boys. People have a good time within such a system. And it's sending a clear and continuous signal to the employees that positive performance is appreciated, recognized, and wanted in the future.

Some of the most successful marketing organizations, like Mary Kay Cosmetics or Amway, using this principle alone, have been able to get dramatic and remarkable performance. One of the interesting findings in the Peters and Waterman book *In Search of Excellence* was that every one of the excellent companies had a "rich reward system." And by "rich" they meant varied, spicy, attractive, attention-grabbing. Is that kind of thing going on in your outfit?

Another aspect of the behavioral consequences discussion concerns disciplinary procedures. What happens to me if my performance deteriorates? Will I receive a talking to, or will people just remain silent and start generating negative feelings about me? Some organizations make a real attempt to let people know exactly where they stand when they're in trouble. I'm not suggesting that that ought to be the only thing management communicates, but I do think employees need to hear it if they are in fact on the carpet.

If you're thinking about how to manipulate rewards, you also ought to entertain the notion that it's possible for a person to miss a merit increase or have his or her salary adjusted downward. Compensation management is too limited if a supervisor's only financial option is simply to grant or withhold a salary increase. Reducing salary or job grade ought to be options, too. These are powerful symbols that clearly communicate that an individual is not meeting expectations. And the purpose of this communication is not so much to punish as to help get him established in the proper performance groove.

There can be no management tolerance of mediocrity. The only performance accepted by management should be performance that meets high and positive expectations. People aren't stupid. They're sharp enough to either satisfy management's expectations for them or leave the organization for some place where they're more comfortable. I'm not suggesting, however, that managers express their intolerance for mediocrity by walking around the office carrying a stick or hassling people, like Rambo in pinstripes. Nobody named us queen for a day, or God. It also doesn't mean that a person who fails to perform in quite the right way is bad or that we have to prove he is wrong. It may be nothing more than a poor fit between a particular person and a particular job. Our job in management is simply to spell out where the boundaries are, indicate what works within this set of circumstances, and clearly communicate that through effective management of positive and negative consequences.

Summary

If we can select good people, give them the orientation they need, provide the supervisory bonding they require, use those people positively, continue to stretch them through professional and educational growth experiences, give them lots of feedback, provide avenues for handling their personal problems, and then, finally, control positive and negative consequences as a powerful, ongoing reinforcement mechanism, it is reasonable for us to expect that they will perform. Is there a guarantee that they won't become problem employees? No.

But if, with no professionalism, we select people cavalierly, let them wander around in a disoriented state, assign them to Bill Fladhammer, who hasn't made a contribution in management in ten years, and we don't match people's skills with the demands of the job, thereby underutilizing them, give neither encouragement nor opportunity for new learning, provide no feedback, allow no avenues for personal-problem handling, and make no effort to match rewards to performance — the result of all that *is* guaranteed. Some call it failure. It might more aptly be termed management malpractice.

5

I Hate Performance Appraisal

There probably isn't a topic that nettles and annoys more managers than the subject of performance appraisal. When I was a young personnel department staffer, just starting out in industry, I recall how difficult it was to get managers to fill out the forms. They would delay returning the forms to the personnel department, and we had to continually monitor and follow up in order to get managers to submit them. When the forms were returned, they were often poorly filled out, or the managers would put down exactly the same things they had the year before. It's probably fair to say that managers never feel more listless or uninterested than when performance appraisals have to be done.

In following up with some of these managers, I noticed that they showed a good deal of resistance and negativism upon being asked even to do this task. In my naïveté, I thought these must be old Neanderthals who were simply dragging their feet in the mud, unwilling to do the obviously necessary and right thing. These hundreds of managers were clearly out of step, clearly incorrect in their perception. These hundreds of managers who didn't want to go along with personnel policy clearly didn't understand the real world.

Or did they?

Why Managers Hate Performance Appraisal

In seminars all across North America, I've had the opportunity to listen carefully to managers' reasons why they don't like doing performance appraisals. As a matter of fact, as an educator, I've found there is no way at all that I can even get them to sit still and consider new ways of doing performance appraisal until I've given them a chance to blow off steam and vent their negative feelings about this process. Here are the kinds of responses managers give for why they don't like doing performance evaluation:

1. I hate playing God. It puts me in a role of judging the person, and that damages our normal working relationship.
2. How can you handle the old-timers? They've been in the same job for 20 years, and there's nothing new you can say about them.
3. My subordinates just see their job differently than I do. It becomes an argument between us as to whose perception is more correct.
4. The process of performance evaluation is too formal. Filling out all those silly forms is a pretense and artificial.
5. A lot of the items in the performance review system don't seem to have any relationship at all to the job this individual is doing.
6. How can I rate a new person? I don't even know this individual yet.
7. The form is no darn good. It's too complicated (too obtuse, too long, too short, too inappropriate).
8. I don't like the timing. They always ask me to do this before we do the salary review. My people don't even listen to what I'm saying. They're listening for only one thing: whether or not they're going to get a raise.
9. I'm uncomfortable. It makes me feel inadequate. It's a job I don't do very often, and I don't like feeling less than confident.
10. There are too many confrontations built into doing performance review.
11. They ask me to review this person's performance for the last year. I can't even remember what happened two months ago.
12. I'm starting below zero, because most employees have a negative attitude toward performance appraisal; they don't like the process.
13. It's too subjective. My version of "attitude," "interpersonal cooperation," and the like is very different from Mary's.
14. I'm afraid of it. It's going to lead to arguments and lawsuits.
15. I don't like the negative impact it has on people. I even heard of an employee who said he was going to commit suicide over his review.

Should Managers Be Listened To?

I notice several things about the foregoing list of managers' complaints. First, I notice that it's a long list. There are not just a few reasons, but lots of reasons, why managers dislike performance appraisal. The second thing I notice about their comments is that they are very specific. They not only don't like this task, they know exactly why they don't like it.

And so I finally got wise. Maybe the rest of the world was not out of step. Maybe all of these tough-minded managers, out of their own direct experience, know something that needs to be listened to—namely, that performance evaluation, as it is typically practiced in American organizations, just does not work and is not worth the time. Maybe, just maybe, all these decision makers were victims of a meaningless and largely worthless pile of work, and their resistance to it was a sure indication that it shouldn't be done.

I've pursued that thought with more than a few audiences and suggested, in fact, that if the list of complaints is that long, and if the appraisal process does not serve managers' interests, disrupts working relationships, and causes negative emotional reactions, maybe we should not do performance appraisal at all. The typical response I get is an immediate round of applause.

The Real Reasons for Doing Performance Review

Then some timorous soul in the back of the room will raise his or her hand and say, "But there are some things that we *do* need from performance review." "What are those?" I ask. The discussion then takes a new turn. Here are some of the typical kinds of responses managers give me for why they think that, in spite of all its faults, performance review is worth doing:

1. The employee wants to know, needs to know, and has a legitimate right to know the answer to the perennial question, "How am I doing?"
2. In some busy units, the performance appraisal sessions may be the only time we have to talk about the job and things that need to be done to improve it. It's the only time I have to find out what is really going in that job or with that person.
3. It's an opportunity to talk about ways to develop this person.
4. Performance appraisal may help control: control of quality, control of performance, control of output.
5. In our organization, it's the only tool we have that allows us to assess talent for promotion and transfer and to get a handle on each person's potential.
6. It may give us some additional basis for making salary administration decisions.
7. It's a chance to solicit ideas and even enhance our interpersonal relationship if it's approached correctly.

Notice what is interesting about this list of managers' reasons for supporting performance review is that the list is very specific. It's also a substantially shorter list than the list of complaints about the process. The list is primarily future-oriented rather than focusing on past performance. And it reflects far less emotional turmoil and anxiety.

Some Systems Are Worse Than No System at All

I submit that performance evaluation as it is done in a majority of corporations is not worth doing. I submit that any system that does not serve the needs of its managers and creates so much resistance is in fact a bad system dreaded by its users. I further submit that unless a performance review system can generate positive acceptance by the manager group, it is a system that is bound to fail.

There is also a growing body of evidence that many performance evaluation systems are not valid and put organizations at legal risk in the area of equal employment opportunity. But I don't think those issues are nearly as important as the one nobody ever talks about—that performance evaluation, as it's currently practiced in most places, just has not done the job of winning management support, has a negative impact on the workforce, accomplishes virtually nothing, and should be discontinued.

I have also learned, though, that managers are not against the concept, only the present approach. They are not against an approach that will accomplish the positive things they're interested in: helping people, getting a handle on what's happening, providing feedback. It's been interesting to me to see that the same managers who speak so negatively about performance review systems are just as quick to suggest criteria for designing a positive system.

Performance appraisal is, of course, applicable to all employees—not only the problem people who are the focus of this book. But an effective system of performance review (and of planned performance, the subject of the next chapter) is particularly critical when you are trying to turn losers into winners.

Is It Legal? Is It True?

Before we turn our attention to an in-depth look at a positive performance review system, let's look at some additional factors that have to be considered. Is the performance review system legal, and is it true, or valid?

A number of legal constraints apply to performance review systems in the United States. The following paragraphs, and the expanded discussion of legal issues in Chapter 13, offer a brief summary of basic guidelines and issues an employer must consider as of this writing. *I strongly recommend that you consult a qualified attorney for expert, up-to-date advice* before implementing a plan in your organization. If your firm operates outside the United States, you should consult local counsel to ensure compliance with the laws of the country involved.

In the United States, the Federal Uniform Guidelines on Employee Selection Procedures, which took effect in September 1978, constitute a central reference for the major requirements with which performance evaluation systems must comply. The guidelines apply not only to selection but to the broader issue of how human performance can be managed and monitored within the organization. They are the law of the land and stem in part from a U.S. Supreme Court decision, *Briggs* v. *Duke Power Company.* These original guidelines have been extensively revised and enlarged in the intervening years.

Under the guidelines, one or the other of the following two criteria must be satisfied in all personnel processes, including processes that affect the utilization of people at work:

1. There must be *no adverse impact* on any of the groups covered by the law: members of a particular race, sex, religion, or national origin, among other categories. That is, if a covered group, by virtue of any personnel practice, like performance appraisal, is negatively affected (performance reviews could prevent promotion, placement, salary increase, or development opportunity), that practice will be held to be illegal unless the following provision applies.
2. Measures or systems that do have an adverse impact must be *shown to be valid*. For example, if an organization holds that a given reading level is required to do certain jobs, then it's conceivable that there might be a negative adverse impact on a protected group. If this matter came before a court, the organization would have to show that the specified reading level is a valid, true, and necessary requirement of the job. In other words, discrimination against protected groups is allowable, as long as the discriminating variable is legitimately related to the truth of the work situation.

In plain English, what these requirements mean for performance evaluation is that any performance review system in which members of a particular race, religion, sex, or other protected group receive lower ratings would be judged to have caused adverse impact. As an example, suppose a manager subconsciously gives lower performance ratings to the women in his unit. He has adversely affected their ability to get better job assignments and higher wages in the future. Any organization that found this to be happening would have two options. One is to eliminate or modify the decision process or criterion that produced the adverse impact — in this case, tell the manager to get his act together. Or the company could, if the circumstances of the case were different, attempt to show that the decisions made by the manager were valid. If a job that women were not considered for had a requirement for lifting heavy loads, then the court would probably hold that the requirement was valid, particularly if the manager's decisions were based on a test or a physician's rating of strength rather than being purely subjective.

In recent years, the absence of adverse impact has become much more difficult to prove. There are simply more and more covered categories being established in court rulings. These include not only race, sex, national origin, and ethnic group but also handicaps, arrest records, military records, religion, religious practice, marital status, age, height, and weight. In some instances, it has also been found to be illegal to discriminate against males with long hair, aliens, or homosexuals. In the future, we are liable to see lawsuits filed on behalf of bald people, or even ugly people!

Because the Federal Uniform Guidelines cover all personnel decisions, that means there are more and more ways to disciminate, including hiring, promotion, demotion, membership, referrals, salary, selection for training, and transfer. The performance review system is central to nearly all of these personnel processes. In order for an organization to show no adverse impact, it would be necessary to prove that no protected group is discriminated against in any personnel decision, an almost impossible task.

Another trend that is making adverse impact harder and harder to deal with is the fact that we're seeing more and more reverse-discrimination claims. For example, as organizations have attempted to redress wrongs against particular racial groups, the racial majority has gone to court to show that it is being discriminated against. As a result, the absence of adverse impact becomes increasingly difficult to prove. An organization either has to abandon the practices in question or establish beyond doubt that they are valid. Proving validity, then, will become the major concern in the future in dealing with the adverse-impact issue.

Demonstrating Validity

Without getting overly technical, there are three approaches to statistical validation that an employer can use:

1. *Prove content validity.* Commonly referred to as face validity, content validity attempts to show a relationship between test scores and key skills needed in significant parts of the job — for example, a typing test for a secretary. If the job candidate can't type, an employer is justified in not giving him or her a position that calls for a lot of typing. On the face of this situation, it is apparent that the person simply cannot do the job.
2. *Prove construct validity.* This shows the relationship between test scores and psychological traits needed on the job, such as leadership skills in a supervisor. Construct validity is sometimes very difficult to show, because so many behaviors go into leadership and other higher-order tasks.
3. *Prove criterion-related validity.* This shows the relationship between test scores and measures of job performance. Industrial psychologists, statisticians, and human resources people have expended a great deal of effort, much of it fruitless, in their attempts to demonstrate criterion validity — to come up with proof or evidence that they are using valid systems, ones based on real job requirements. The issue of criterion validity has been particularly important in such systems as performance review.

So How Valid Are Performance Appraisals?

The bottom line in terms of our discussion of performance appraisal is this: The studies that have been done of performance review and personal appraisal systems show that they often have little if any validity. Let me state that again: It has been virtually impossible to demonstrate validity; performance evaluation systems are just not very truthful or accurate measures — precisely what managers have been complaining about for years!

Among other things, studies have shown that an average employee's merit rating varies by level of job status, age, and years of service. Middle-aged people in lower grade levels are consistently rated lower than young or old professionals! Constant errors occur across all traits. Some supervisors tend to rate everybody high or everybody low, and some supervisors will rate much higher than other supervisors in the same factory in units doing the same kind of work. These kinds of rating problems are inherent whenever you have a subjective rating system, and that's exactly what performance review is. This is not say that evaluation systems have no value, but the extent to which they are fraught with problems from legal, statistical, and managerial-acceptance standpoints seriously impairs their usefulness as instruments of applied measurement.

Nor is the concern about the limitations and problems of personal and performance evaluation systems a recent phenomenon. Such issues were prophetically addressed more than 20 years ago by Dr. Robert Guion. Since then, the courts have largely supported his views:

> Many of the appraisals, however, are so poorly done that they are inadequate for either [administrative purposes or criterion measures]. Two major limitations are common: (1) the unwillingness of the executive doing the appraisal to be frank in ratings that he must later discuss with the person being evaluated, and (2) the lack of relevance of the ratings themselves.[1]

> Personal appraisal programs are open to . . . major criticisms. The first and most basic is . . . the absence of adequate validation . . . most personal appraisal programs not only are not validated but lack even evidence of concern for relevance.[2]

Now, I'll quickly summarize what's been said thus far. Managers don't like doing performance review because existing systems just don't work for them. Yet the same managers see and understand the need for some mechanism that would aid communication and other coordination and control processes that are necessary for people to work together.

The second thing I indicated is that the law is placing increasing constraints on such personnel systems as performance review. The law requires that either an employer must show no adverse impact, or if there is adverse impact, the employer must show validation.

The third point is that existing performance review systems, almost without exception, are invalid in a statistical and legal sense. Therefore, they are very hard to defend, as are the decisions influenced by them. So, both from a legal perspective and from managers' commonsense point of view, performance review is highly suspect as it is now done.

What Can a Manager Do?

A manager responds: "Well, all of this certainly sounds important, and I'm glad to have the information. I'm also overwhelmed and absolutely confused as to just what I ought to do!'' I think any manager who doesn't feel somewhat confused and intimidated by this topic doesn't understand the situation! And while this manual is not designed to provide a complete treatment of the subject of performance appraisal, allow me to get down to brass tacks in terms of what a manager can do.

Basically, there are two approaches to performance evaluation that ought to be considered, both of which will satisfy most of the legal requirements and also overcome most of the criticisms that managers express. Those two approaches are self-rating (discussed in the balance of this chapter) and planned performance (discussed in the following chapter).

The Case for Self-Rating in Performance Evaluation

The first of these better approaches requires that managers move toward a participative method for performance review in which employees rate their own performance and then review that rating with their boss. The boss, of course, retains veto power and can change the rating to whatever the situation calls for. Participative performance evaluation doesn't mean that the boss surrenders his or her authority, but it does mean that this is a task that can and should be partially delegated to the employee.

Now, suppose we gave a hundred employees an opportunity to fill out their own performance review. What would they do? Some would rate themselves at about the same level that their boss would. Some would tend to rate themselves higher than their boss would, and some would rate themselves lower than their boss would. What percentage of employees do you guess would tend to rate themselves at or below the level at which their boss would rate them? Would you believe 90 percent? This astounding phenomenon of accurate or low rating behavior was first discovered in college courses where professors sometimes gave students the opportunity to submit their own grade. At first, it was thought that a bunch of high-achieving, aggressive young people would tend to overrate, but in fact, the majority rated themselves at or below the level that the professor would. The same proportion of accurate raters and over- or underraters has been found at work, and this general rule makes the whole idea of self-rating worth considering.

Now, let's examine the 90 percent further, because nothing is ever absolutely perfect in management, and we're looking for systems that will work for most managers, most of the time. What does a supervisor say to somebody who has rated himself or herself lower than the supervisor would? Obviously, such employees are very hard on themselves, very self-critical. I think we all sometimes tend to be more critical of ourselves than we are of others. We know our own failings, our deficiencies, and we are very mindful of these, to such an extent that we become almost unable to see our strengths. To the employee who rated himself or herself lower on the typical evaluation form, the manager says:

> I'm sorry, Betty, I must change your rating. I don't agree with it, and I think that you're producing far more than you think, the quality of your work is better, and your cooperation higher than you've given yourself credit for.

And so, the manager's role is that of taking this person with a low self-perception and raising that perception. And what's the impact on the employee? The employee thinks the manager is a god! The manager is a hero, a praiser, an encourager, a raiser-upper. In practice, managers report that dealing this way with employees who have underrated themselves generates a profoundly positive attitude toward the boss and the evaluation, as well as a heightened sense of respect and mutual openess. The boss has a legitimate reason to praise and to increase the rating of this person. In other words, you don't lose with this type of person by raising the rating, and the impact of doing so is far greater than if the manager had completed the form without letting the employee participate.

What about an employee who rated himself or herself about where the manager would? How does the manager respond?

> Well, Tom, I think you have accurate self-knowledge. You obviously are in tune with what's going on, and I want to tell you that I pretty much see the job the way you've outlined it here. I am going to change a thing a two and add a couple of comments, but I think you're just about on target.

Keep in mind that employees who rate themselves at the same level the manager would aren't necessarily rating themselves high. They could be rating themselves low or only average. Nonetheless, such employees are showing that they have good self-perception, that they understand where they are. This is important knowledge for their manager to gain regarding them. Managers state that when dealing with people who rated themselves accurately, they don't lose by indicating their agreement with these people. Here, the manager's role becomes that of a confirmer, a reinforcer of where such employees are now. And, report managers, that provides an opportunity to chat with them about "Where do we want to go from here? What now? What next?"

Notice that the manager wins with both of these groups — with 90 percent of the people. If you ask managers, "Are you winning with 90 percent of your employees using the traditional performance review approach, where you tell them what the ratings are?" the answer would be an emphatic *no!* So, even at this point, it is easy to see that the self-rating system seems to be a better performer.

What About the 10 Percent?

Now, what about those who rate themselves higher than where the manager would have put them? That group breaks down into two parts. About 5 percent of the people have rated themselves too high not because they're trying to play games with the manager but because they really believe that their performance deserves the rating they've given it. Here, the manager says:

> I'm sorry, Jeff, I don't see it quite that way. I want to tell you that there have been some problems and also some milestones that you haven't yet achieved. The way I

see your present performance doesn't put you at that level yet, but I know you have potential. There's no question in my mind that you're going to be there one day, but right now I have to lower this rating a little. I don't want you to be discouraged by that, because I'm here to help you get to that point, and even surpass it.

What's the response of people who have honestly rated themselves too high but who then learn from their boss that they have not yet achieved that level? Well, sometimes there's a little embarrassment, sometimes there's a little apology, and sometimes there's a subsequent growth opportunity, particularly when the supervisor has presented his or her response kindly. You really don't lose with these people either. At heart, they are good people who aren't there to fight you about the rating, but who simply had a different perception, and now they understand how their boss sees it.

Finally, we come to the troubled 5 percent who have also rated themselves too high. Often they have inflated opinions of themselves and will want to use this opportunity to provoke an argument. They are ready to defend their viewpoint versus their manager's viewpoint. Does the manager win with these people? Usually not. Would the manager have won with them if he or she had done the rating first? No, because some folks will never be happy with having their performance rated, no matter who does it.

Testing the Concept

Keeping in mind the concept of self-evaluation, let's return for a moment to the list of criticisms that managers reported about the present evaluation system. One of their complaints was that filling out the forms takes too much time. Note that the manager has now delegated the task of form completion to the employees. Manager time is slashed. Employees by and large do not mind filling out the form themselves, since it's obviously in their best interest.

What about managers' distaste for "playing God?" Do they still have that role under this kind of approach? No, because the dynamics of the situation shift dramatically. A manager, by delegating the task, is basically saying to the employee:

> Look, you're responsible for the work, and you're responsible for rating how well the work is coming along. That's just part of the job. And you're the pro, the expert. I'm not going to be monitoring you like a little child. I expect you to be an adult and candidly report what's going on.

That approach treats people like grown-ups, and they don't feel as if they're being graded. As a result, they have a whole different set of feelings about this process. Managers complained that, under the old system, they felt they were being judgmental and that it was destructive of their working relationship with their subordinates. Note that under the self-review and self-appraisal process, employees take responsibility for themselves. So the role of the boss changes to that of coach and teacher and counselor.

In like fashion, as one goes down the list of objections that managers expressed, one finds that virtually all those objections are either resolved or minimized under the self-review process. Just changing who does the rating eliminates most of the reasons why managers resist. I've seen this process, this changeover, within organizations, and I tell you that it's dramatic and that managers who had fought performance evaluation now welcome it.

Let's carry the critique of this process one step further by considering self-rating in light of the legal concerns over adverse impact and validity. And let's assume a worst-case scenario in which, for whatever reason, the employer has been taken to court over some issue connected with performance evaluation. The employer's legal position is greatly strengthened if its attorney can submit performance reviews that were filled out and signed by the employee, saying, "Your Honor, we didn't rate the employee this way; we simply confirmed the rating that the employee gave to himself."

Under the old evaluation system, the company and manager had to prove that their rating was valid. Under the new system, the onus shifts to the disgruntled employee. The fact is that far fewer cases have landed in court when employees have such a direct hand in monitoring and evaluating their own performance than when these tasks are done solely by the supervisor.

Yes, But . . .

Allow me to anticipate some objections and questions. The self-rating idea is such a simple one, and like just about everything else in management, the simpler the idea is, the better it seems to work. However, there are some caveats and some application guidelines that are worth considering.

Sometimes not all employees are comfortable in filling out the form. If so, you might consider continuing to do direct supervisory rating for those people. In other cases, it's been reported that some employees lack adequate reading or writing skills. You might want to consider the idea of letting them think their rating through at home and then come in for a meeting in which you act as the scribe and write down what they tell you. Then you could discuss it with them. Or you might decide to do a supervisory rating on them, too. So use the self-assessment concept as a tool, but adapt it to fit your own particular situation.

My observation is that once a manager starts accepting the idea that performance review really isn't part of his job, but that performance coaching and development of people are, then the issue of who ought to fill out the form becomes very minor. I believe that if you'll think this through, you'll start to move away from the old, outmoded, and invalid system toward a system that reflects the new American organization and the new participative model that has worked so well for the Japanese, who have used self-evaluation ever since World War II with outstanding success.

Just consider what's been happening in Japan during the last 40 years under participative approaches. Japanese management has been telling its employees that they have direct responsibility for themselves, their jobs, and everything that happens in the organization. Participative performance review systems simply reinforce that message. Meanwhile, in North America, where this concept originated, during the last 40 years we've seen managements continuing to fight with unions, continuing to guarantee management prerogatives, and continuing to tell employees: "Here's what your performance rating is. We're going to treat you like children for the rest of your life." You judge the productivity track record and tell me if that antiquated philosophy yields the kind of results you want.

Another guideline for application is to confront the argument that somehow all we need is a better form. I have seen about 600 different performance review forms. I've never found one that I like in all respects. There's no magic in the form. The real purpose of performance review is for boss and employee to have an opportunity to discuss how things are going and how to make things better. I don't think the paper ever accomplishes that. It's just a record, a place to put down in writing where we think things are at a given moment in time. We need to have such a record, and the forms provided in Chapter 6 are the best I know. Use them, or adapt them, and don't waste a lot of time on forms design. Instead, get on with the job of communication. If certain divisions or certain departments want to use one form and others want to use another form, fine, as long as there's nothing illegal about any of them.

One thing I would suggest, though, in the forms-design area is to get rid of any personality-oriented rating words such as *initiative, cooperation, enthusiasm,* or *attitude.* If you really want to look foolish, go sit in a courtroom and have some attorney examine your qualifications as a psychologist: "Exactly how big, Mr. Johnson, would you say an attitude is? Have you ever seen an attitude? Does one glow in the dark? Is it oblong?" Trying to evaluate personality with words that have very little connection with measurable events is risky at best and foolish at worst. So keep the performance rating form focused on the job, keep it focused on performance, keep it focused on behavior, keep it focused on results.

A lot of performance evaluation forms that I have seen pretty much ask you to summarize everything that's happened in the last year. They're backward-looking. Even if we could get an accurate and valid measure of everything that happened in the last year, who cares? What can you possibly change about the past? The only thing we can really do is learn from the past, so I would suggest that performance review ought to be focused primarily on the future. "This is where things are now, but here's what we're going to do." An ideal performance review form should probably reserve 50 percent of its content for a discussion of what is going to be done in the areas of development, assigning new jobs, or changing job content and what will be done to change the accountabilities and authorities that people now have. Isn't the primary objective of management to make things better? So how managers can help employees improve in the future ought to be the focus of performance evaluation. If we spent our time thinking about that, I believe our organizations would be a lot richer and a lot better off.

Employees can't change the past. They may have been losers in the past; their performance may have been dismal in the past. But even after you rate that and prove it, so what? It's still only history—a dead issue. Do you have a bigger market share because of it? Have you got more profit on the bottom line, higher productivity, better team interaction? I doubt it. So let's keep our performance reviews focused on performance, not on personalities. Let's keep them focused on the future, not on the past. Let's keep them oriented toward valid, concrete, relevant issues rather than toward subjective concepts. And let's keep in mind that there's no magic in the form, only in the process of two people trying to work together to create a better future.

Summary

No doubt about it: Existing performance appraisal systems are almost universally disliked. Managers' reactions to them range from avoidance of the task to outright hostility. They offer a lengthy, specific, *and convincing* list of reasons to justify their dislike, too.

On the other hand, managers can also whip off a list of equally convincing reasons why some sort of performance review does need to be done. These reasons reveal that the managers' quarrel is not with the performance appraisal concept itself but rather with the fundamentally useless systems so often found in today's organizations. Some of these systems are worse than useless, actually harming working relationships and putting firms at legal risk.

The issues of legality and validity are relevant both to existing performance review systems and to any new system that might be proposed. Basically, to be legal, an evaluation system must not adversely impact any of the growing number of groups protected by the law, or if it does, the system must be shown to be valid—that is, its provisions must be legitimately job-related.

When considered from the standpoint of legality and validity (to say nothing of managerial acceptance), present performance evaluation systems simply don't measure up.

The best alternative is performance evaluation through self-rating. It has been found that a surprising 90 percent of employees are realistic in their self-assessments, or even overly hard on themselves. Of the remaining 10 percent who rate themselves higher than their managers would have done, about half are honestly mistaken and gracefully accept the managers' constructive reassessment; the other half are the argumentative minority who could be expected to persist in their inflated opinions of themselves regardless of the merits of the evaluation system.

Putting the performance evaluation ball in the employees' court in this fashion not only satisfies nearly all the complaints managers express about the present evaluation process; the self-rating system holds up better in court, as well.

In revitalizing the performance evaluation system, managers must ignore the trivial details of forms design and abandon the assessment of such intangible qualities as "enthusiasm" and "personality," concentrating instead on a future-oriented, participative approach that will yield results.

In the next chapter, we will turn our attention to the second major approach to performance review, which I call planned performance.

6

But I Love
Planned Performance

Work planning is a system that goes beyond performance evaluation. It is a management by objectives system, but one without a lot of the extra paperwork and deadweight usually associated with poorly designed MBO approaches. It is a very powerful and practical tool for managers and is ideally suited both for preventing problem employees and for channeling and controlling employee behavior that has gotten off track.

The system relies on two forms, one that sets out the work plan and one that reviews performance and plans for development. (A sample of each form is shown on pages 72–73 and 76–77.) Some organizations will use this approach instead of a separate evaluation process; others will tack on a formal performance evaluation instrument to summarize the quarterly performance plans. As you review the forms, their use will become more apparent. While not for everybody, they do work very well for professional, technical, and managerial employees. These forms and the related text were developed by the author as part of a program called The Integrated Management System, code-named MANSYS.*

Part 1: Work Planning and Specification

The objective of the Work Planning & Specification form is to delineate exactly what each job position is all about and set in motion a quarterly work plan that will clearly specify what is to be accomplished during the period. As Peter Drucker wrote, "One either manages by objectives, or one does not manage."

The form is filled out by individual associates (subordinates) and reviewed by the

---

* MANSYS: ©1986 by Dr. V. Clayton Sherman, Management House, Inc., Inverness, Illinois.

manager. Differences of opinion are then negotiated in a joint meeting. The amount of preparation time will vary by the job, but the form usually takes the associate one to two hours to complete. The review time with the manager typically averages 30 to 60 minutes per associate in the first cycle, less time thereafter.

The form seems to be most appropriate and works best when the associate is another supervisor or a professional or technical person. The form is not as appropriate for highly routine jobs or jobs that have a number of continuously recycling duties, such as clerical positions. However, it should be pointed out that actual field experience with the instrument showed that a number of hourly and clerical employees offered the opportunity to manage their jobs in this fashion were quite enthused. The general rule of application regarding who should be covered by MANSYS probably needs to take into account the interest and capabilities of the individual. So exceptions are encouraged, and experimenting with the tool is a good idea until such time as the manager sees how best to relate it to his or her own unit's needs.

Guide to the Form

The reader should now refer to the Work Planning & Specification form while reading the following detailed instructions.

A. Position Focus

Position focus is designed to clearly identify the major objectives or results that this particular job is to accomplish. Many job descriptions become lengthy recitals of various tasks and duties rather than a specification of what the job actually consists of.

Key Functions/Responsibilities. Some salary systems, such as the Hay salary system, produce job descriptions that include at their end a listing of four to eight "principal accountabilities." If your organization is currently operating with focused job descriptions that produce core accountability statements, these can be entered under the column headed "Key Functions/Responsibilities." If that information has not been determined, then the following MANSYS list of key result areas could be entered.

There are seven key result areas (KRAs) that are relevant to every manager's job and are to a large degree relevant to many professional and technical positions:

- □ *Customer satisfaction.* The customer is that individual or group of people who are the direct recipients of the services provided by this position. In some cases, this may be an outside, paying customer. In some cases, such as in a staff department, the customer might be other line managers or company personnel. Finding out what the customer needs, and satisfying those needs, is a key result area.
- □ *Economic Health.* Nearly every job has a measurable financial impact: sales, expense control, or profitability. The economic lifeblood of the organization is a concern for every manager.
- □ *Innovation.* Finding new and better ways to do things is absolutely necessary in an ever changing, dynamic business environment. It is not uncommon for managers to complain that their employees often don't seem to provide them with

ideas or suggestions. Through MANSYS, innovation can be clearly stated as a key function and responsibility of the job.

- □ *Quality.* Quality of product or service is a concern of every position. The market does not want junk. How to maintain or improve quality standards is an essential result area.
- □ *Productivity.* Maximizing output given the amount of input resources available is a key component of most jobs. To improve organizational efficiency or systematize work flow is a key result.
- □ *People growth.* Contributing to the growth of our associates and growing ourselves are major results needed for many jobs and are a prime requirement for all supervisory positions.
- □ *Organization climate.* Improving the "feel of the place," the working atmosphere, or the corporate/unit culture is always a must.

If the job description or the KRAs listed above do not adequately cover the focus of the job, then planned performance will have served its first purpose, by helping the manager think through why this job exists at all.

Weight. The second column under "Position Focus" asks for a percentage weighting for each of the position's major responsibilities. One entry may be worth 10 percent of the job, another 25 percent, yet another 40 percent.

In a study done at General Electric, it was found that less than half of the manager-associate pairs could agree on 50 percent of the job elements. In Figure 2, the associate described his job as comprising elements represented by the upper block. But the manager thinks that the associate should be doing a different cluster of activities, represented by the lower block. Where these two boxes overlap, there is agreement and congruence. In these areas, the associate is doing what the manager thinks he or she should be doing.

But the associate also thinks he should be doing some other things, which causes the manager to wonder why the associate is doing those things and not the things the manager had intended. The expectations that each has for the job, if left unmanaged, lead to blind alleys, the performance of unnecessary work, failure to perform desired work, and ultimately, frustration and conflict between the pair. The first function of

Figure 2. Comparison between an associate's view of his job and the manager's view of that job.

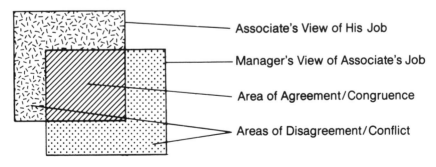

PLANNED PERFORMANCE: WORK PLANNING &

MANSYS℠ **THE INTEGRATED MANAGEMENT SYSTEM**

A. POSITION FOCUS		B. WORK PLAN
KEY FUNCTIONS/RESPONSIBILITIES (WHAT'S THE JOB?)	WEIGHT (WHAT %?)	PROJECTS/OBJECTIVES (WHAT'S TO BE DONE?)

Additional copies are available. For information, write to Dr. V. Clayton Sherman, c/o AMACOM Books, 135 W. 50th St., New York, N.Y. 10020.

SPECIFICATION

ASSOCIATE _____ TITLE _____

MANAGER _____ DATE _____

	PRIORITY (A-B-C)	AUTHORITY (A-B-C)	SCHEDULING			RESULTS/STANDARDS OF PERFORMANCE (HOW WILL RESULTS BE JUDGED?)
			START	REVIEW	COMPLETE	

planned performance is to reach agreement on exactly what job the incumbent is to do and how much time and effort he should be expending in doing it.

B. Work Plan

The "Work Plan" portion of the planned performance program is designed to list the specific projects or tasks that will be undertaken in the current quarter. While the form can be completed on an as-needed basis, experience suggests that sitting down with some discipline every 90 days and mapping out a specific work plan makes the most sense.

Projects/Objectives. On a mechanical level, the form allows as much room as necessary under this column for each item. More than one box can be filled in in order to list the projects and objectives associated with a particular position function/responsibility. Generally, the projects/objectives statements should be brief and not overly detailed but should nonetheless be specific enough to identify exactly what kind of work is to be done.

Priority. This column asks for an agreement between the manager and associate regarding how much priority a particular project should be given. The priority code is:

A = *Immediate priority.* High priority that is due to either importance or urgency.
B = *Intermediate priority.* Average importance.
C = *Lowest priority.* To be undertaken only after projects having A and B priorities are completed.

A little thinking through the priority codes at this point will prevent a lot of problems at the end of the 90-day period in terms of associates and managers getting out of sync with each other regarding the relative importance rating of the projects.

Authority. Another common complaint heard in the workplace is, "They give me the responsibility but not the authority." Confusion about the degree of authority an associate has to carry out a task is a major stumbling block and can easily be handled by entering authority codes:

A = *Complete authority.* The associate has full authority to proceed and carry out the project and does not need to report back. In most jobs, about 85 percent of the work being done by an experienced associate should have an A level of authority.
B = *Do and report.* The associate has full authority to act, but the manager requires some feedback about what has transpired. This may be due to political considerations or the need to integrate with other ongoing work. For experienced people, about 10 percent of the tasks will be Bs.
C = *Discuss first, then do.* The associate definitely will have authority to carry out the task, but the manager requests that there be a discussion prior to the associate's starting the work. This could be due to its difficult or sensitive nature. C = level authority will constitute approximately 5 percent of the assigned tasks for experienced people.

Scheduling. Dates can be entered for the anticipated start and completion of each project. Also, review dates for intermediate monitoring can be entered, depending on the nature of the project. All three columns may be useful. In other cases, managers will only want to enter the dates of completion. As with all other aspects of MANSYS, only those portions should be used that are helpful to the work team.

Results/Standards of Performance. This column provides an opportunity to specify how results will be judged. In some cases, it may be possible to enter a quantifiable number (sales volume, budget limits, a reject percentage, and so on). In other cases, particularly in some areas involving staff or qualitative work, it may only be possible to judge results on a subjective basis. The manager's opinion, the associate's opinion, or approval from an executive committee are acceptable and valid measures.

Part 2: Review, Redirection, and Development

The Review, Redirection & Development form is a continuation of the planned performance program and is completed at the *end* of the quarter or operating period. It is organized in the manager's system binder as a facing page for the first sheet used in the process on the Work Planning & Specification form. The Review, Redirection & Development form allows the manager to compare the specific tasks that were planned at the beginning of the quarter, and documented on the Work Planning & Specification form, with the actual performance outcome. As with the Work Planning & Specification form, the associate prepares the Review, Redirection & Development form for his manager's review.

Guide to the Form

C. Progress Review

Rating Results. The associate enters a rating for the results achieved on the particular project or objective according to the following code:

0 = No problem — project accomplished satisfactorily or appropriate interim results achieved.
1 = Some problem or difficulty.
2 = Serious problem or difficulty.

In essence, this is the evaluation completed by the associate on his own performance. He is directly commenting on progress made on specific work assignments. Note, too, how naturally this system flows out of the quarterly work plan.

Subsequent/Corrective Action. The associate enters the subsequent action that needs to be taken. In some cases, this will be a continuation of ongoing work, a

PLANNED PERFORMANCE: REVIEW, REDIRECTION
MANSYS℠ **THE INTEGRATED MANAGEMENT SYSTEM**

C. PROGRESS REVIEW				
RATING RESULTS (0-1-2) ASSOC.	MGR.	TOTAL	**SUBSEQUENT/CORRECTIVE ACTION** (WHERE DO WE GO FROM HERE?)	**MANAGER SUPPORT** (HOW CAN MANAGER HELP?)

Additional copies are available. For information, write to Dr. V. Clayton Sherman, c/o AMACOM Books, 135 W. 50th St., New York, N.Y. 10020.

PLANNED PERFORMANCE
PART 11—REVIEW, REDIRECTION & DEVELOPMENT

& DEVELOPMENT

ASSOCIATE _____ TITLE _____

MANAGER _____ DATE _____

D. DEVELOPMENT PLAN

DEVELOPMENT NEED (ASSOC. OR GROUP) (WHAT SKILLS/CAPABILITIES NEEDED?)	DEVELOPMENT ACTION (HOW STRETCH?)	RESPONSIBILITY (WHO DOES WHAT?)	SCHEDULING START	REVIEW	COMPLETE
		ASSOCIATE			
		MANAGER			
		ASSOCIATE			
		MANAGER			
		ASSOCIATE			
		MANAGER			
		ASSOCIATE			
		MANAGER			
		ASSOCIATE			
		MANAGER			
		ASSOCIATE			
		MANAGER			
		ASSOCIATE			
		MANAGER			

redirection, or a corrective action required at this time. If there is a problem, the associate has first crack at recommending what should be done. Not only does he rate his own performance but then lays out any prescriptive action. Even if there's a performance problem, the associate still feels ownership and control in fixing it.

Manager Support. The associate also enters the support needed from his manager at this point in the ongoing work flow. The manager then considers the progress review statements made by the associate and enters his own perception of the results obtained thus far, using the same $0 = 1 = 2$ rating code. The associate's and manager's ratings are totaled, with the scores now ranging from 0 to 4. This clarifies the areas in which the manager and associate are in agreement and identifies the areas that are seen quite differently, forming the basis for a discussion of those perceptions.

The manager also reviews the proposed subsequent/corrective actions, endorses or changes them, and adds his own thinking in terms of what further assistance may be necessary.

In the case of an incomplete project, that project is carried forward to the work plan for the following period and is entered as an ongoing item with new scheduling dates, as appropriate. In the case of a major project, it is possible that items may appear on the work plan over a protracted period of time.

D. Development Plan

Development Need. In discussing the progress made on various projects, there will be an opportunity for the manager to see areas where the associate may require further training, development, or coaching. Work discussions may also reveal needs that are common to the entire work group. Under the column headed "Development Need," the associate or manager, as appropriate, can describe the need in terms of the behavioral or attitudinal changes that are required. It is not uncommon for associates, in tackling new projects, to encounter areas requiring new information or skill. This is part of their normal job growth. And before deciding what should be done about this, it is useful to specify the particular skill or capability needed.

Development Action. Here, a specific strategy or prescription for dealing with the development need is sketched out. This may include recommendations from the associate or the manager; in some cases, the expertise of a staff development group may be sought, as well.

Responsibility and Scheduling. This column indicates who is to do what in terms of arranging the development action. In those cases where the appropriate thing to do is simply increased coaching in the unit, this becomes a rather straightforward entry. In other cases, there may be a need to obtain approvals or extra budget authority in order to send people to outside educational programs, and so responsibility is spelled out along with any necessary scheduling.

Excellent companies generally spend more dollars and a larger percentage of the expense budget on training and development activities than do less effective organizations. Further, the best programs relate specific development activity to central job tasks. MANSYS clearly allows that kind of specification.

At the same time, a given development activity will not necessarily be appropriate for every person or project, and it is not uncommon for sections of the development plan to be left blank. Users should not be disturbed by this but rather should anticipate it. Even when a certain section is not used, its presence on the form serves to keep the development issue clearly in front of the work team.

Summary

The planned-performance program is a practical, effective, MBO-based approach for organizing, monitoring, upgrading, and enhancing employee performance. Not only does it expedite getting work done, but it positively controls and channels human performance.

The first part of the program utilizes the Work Planning & Specification form, on which the associate and his manager define what the job consists of and develop a detailed action plan for carrying out the specified job functions.

The second part of the planned-performance program utilizes the Review, Redirection & Development form, on which the associate and his manager assess the associate's progress toward attainment of the objectives that were outlined in the action plan and identify development activities that must be undertaken to upgrade or enhance the associate's or the group's performance.

It should be emphasized that planned performance is a fully participative approach, in which the associate accepts a large share of responsibility for the execution, and the success, of the program. The associate is the one who completes both the Work Planning & Specification form and the Review, Redirection & Development form. Information on these forms is then reviewed jointly by the associate and his manager, to arrive at shared understandings and create action and development plans to which both are committed.

7

Eight Steps to Positive Discipline of Problem Employees

Problem employees generate all kinds of emotional reactions in their supervisors and co-workers. They create a lot of anger, a lot of distrust, a sense of sadness and unhappiness, and some real frustration. It's a natural tendency for many supervisors to want to lash out or punish these people. But that kind of approach is usually going to be counterproductive. The problem is that emotional reactions are futile and punishment usually does not work (at least, its effect isn't very predictable).

Unfortunately, for too many managers, their concept of discipline is to administer some kind of punishment, such as overtime, days off without pay, or the next 26 dirty jobs that come along. But the word *discipline* comes from the word *disciple.* A disciple is a follower, and the goal in discipline is to turn someone who is not following the proper path into a supportive and helpful follower. So I like to think of discipline in this positive sense. The manager doesn't have to get mad, regard this person as an enemy, or set out to "get" the culprit. The approach must be positive; the aim, to make a disciple of this person. Discipline is at heart an educational process. Its intent is to help the potential disciple learn what is expected and how to perform.

When one talks with managers who are wrestling with a problem case, one usually doesn't find an attitude of animosity or a desire to inflict punishment: The manager simply wants the person to get back on the right track. This objective, results-oriented attitude should remind us of what we're really trying to achieve here — getting the work done with the people at hand. That is the whole aim of management, and it is precisely the goal that should guide us in dealing with people when they go astray. The purpose of this segment of our discussion is to provide a philosophy and an operating procedure that will help get people back onto the performance path.

I'm going to present an eight-step process for the positive discipline of problem employees, an overview of which is shown in Figure 3. This action sequence will lead in stepwise fashion to the best solution and prevent a lot of random attempts at coping.

Figure 3. Positive discipline of problem employees.

ANALYZE THE EMPLOYEE'S PERFORMANCE

- Describe it
- Identify its cost
- Gather data
- Consider the possibility of supervisory failings

IMPLEMENT EMPLOYEE-COUNSELING SESSIONS

- Provide positive and negative performance feedback
- Express both displeasure and confidence
- Make counseling sessions a "word to the wise"

DOCUMENT! DOCUMENT! DOCUMENT!

- Report specifics
- Stick to the facts

REVIEW THE SITUATION

- Review the discipline policy
- Consult with human resources development and management
- Develop an action plan
- When you do decide to clean house, act quickly

IMPLEMENT YOUR ACTION AGENDA

- Provide education
- Conduct counseling sessions
- Utilize the employee assistance program
- Issue warnings
- Employ social censure
- Reduce rewards
- Examine the issue of punishment
- Offer support

MONITOR FOR COMPLIANCE

- Conduct a daily/weekly review
- Repeat your efforts, per your judgment, keeping in mind that three tries is usually considered a reasonable maximum

ISSUE A FINAL WARNING

- "Shape up or ship out"

PROCEED WITH TERMINATION/RESIGNATION

Problem employee cases don't respond well to hit-or-miss approaches, but a manager can achieve control when he does this job *by the numbers.*

1. Analyze the Employee's Performance

The first step in positive discipline is to examine the performance of the problem employee. Actually writing down a description of what the manager means by the performance discrepancy is an important beginning. Often supervisors will have a shorthand phrase to describe the employee's problem. One of the most notorious of these is the phrase "bad attitude." Describing exactly what he means by a bad attitude allows the manager to be a little more objective and a lot more specific about how the situation should be dealt with.

Just what does the employee say or do that earns him this "bad attitude" label (or whatever other problem label may be attached)? By the phrase "bad attitude," the supervisor may mean that the employee in question has a negative influence on other employees or engages in side conversations when the manager addresses the unit staff. Or perhaps "bad attitude" means that the employee uses vulgar language. It's impossible to manage an attitude; we can only manage behavior. Making guesses about people's motivation is neither very productive nor very defensible in a court of law. I'm willing to grant that people have bad attitudes, a negative mind-set that is inappropriate at work, but we've got to be more specific and factual than that if we're to get a handle on it. So, in writing, describe exactly what the employee does, what the employee says, and the impact that it has on others.

Writing it down helps the manager's objectivity. It gets the problem out of the manager's head and heart and reduces it to words on paper. Spelling problems out in written reports, on charts, or in proposals for action helps the manager gain effective control over emotion and begin to identify the multitude of variables that are probably operating in the situation.

Next in performance analysis, a manager needs to identify the exact cost or value of the problem behaviors. In some cases, managers report that the employee problem they're dealing with irks and annoys them, but the actual cost of it is not really that great! If that should be the case, the next action step is to rejoice, because you're at the end of the chain! It's not realistic to expect that all your subordinates are going to have personalities that you find pleasing, and if the cost of the problem that they represent is not substantial, count yourself lucky and become a little more tolerant.

This may seem like too simple a point to even mention, but it's been found that sometimes irritating behaviors loom too large in the supervisor's mind. A small annoyance, endured for a long period of time, can assume too much significance. Things do get blown out of proportion. There is so much work to do, so little time to do it in, and sometimes things that we might be more tolerant of in a less stressed environment can start to take center stage in our thinking. If an actual calculation of costs shows that the situation is no big deal, then relax. Neither the world nor the people in it are perfect, and maybe the answer is just to accept life's realities with good grace.

On the other hand, the costs of the problem behavior may be both significant and intolerable and may clearly indicate a need for correction. What are the costs that ought to be calculated? The following are some examples of the kinds of direct financial costs that should be considered:

Lost-time or sick-time payments
Lowered productivity
Cost of errors
Workers' compensation payments and accident-related costs
Impact on other workers' morale
Excessive time demands on the manager

In addition to describing the problem and its costs, the manager should gather data. What specific evidence do we have? What testimony do we have? What reports are available? How much of this is direct observation as opposed to hearsay? So a file must be compiled. This file may or may not be directly used in building a case against the employee, but it is certainly important that the manager get his or her facts together.

The last step I would suggest under performance analysis is for the manager to take a good close look at his *own* performance. The following sorts of questions are relevant: Where have I failed? What have I left undone that I should have done? Is there a possibility that I contributed to this person's failings? Is there anything that I can do, even at this late date, that might turn this person around? Now I don't think managers should get trapped by the "paralysis of analysis," nor do I recommend a guilt trip. But I think its going to be awfully difficult for the manager to confront the other person's failings if his own failings are just as bad.

2. Implement Employee-Counseling Sessions

The next step in the process is to conduct some direct employee-counseling sessions. While this might be handled through the annual performance review, counseling designed to manage problem employees is probably more focused than the annual performance review, more limited in terms of dealing with a specific problem area, and so a separate discussion is usually called for.

In this employee-counseling session, or series of sessions, an attempt should be made to give both positive and negative performance feedback. Some managers make the mistake of simply talking to problem employees about all the things they have done wrong and citing their areas of deficiency. That creates a feeling of defeat in these employees. What is more helpful is to spell out clearly what the person does very well (the positive side of the ledger) and what it is that causes you concern (the negative side of the ledger). In this way, problem employees have a better and more balanced picture of themselves and can see why you are troubled about the negative aspects of their performance given the fact that there are so many positive aspects.

In the course of providing this evenhanded positive and negative performance feedback, and there shouldn't be any game playing. And this session shouldn't be thought of as a highly sophisticated counseling process, just some candid communication:

Manager:	Harriet, I respect your right to think and believe differently than I do about the way things should be done. I believe it helps to have some diversity of opinion around here, and I know that not every good idea will come from me.
	But there's a point beyond which differences of opinion don't help us get the job done, and that point is reached when I make a decision. At that point, things have to be done my way because, right or wrong, it's my responsibility.
Employee:	I understand that. What are you driving at?
Manager:	Just this. Word has reached me that you are disagreeing with my decisions on the new computer procedures, and I've been hearing this from several sources. Is this the case?
Employee:	Well not exactly. Yes, I've said some things, but not to undermine you. Say, who are these people anyway?
Manager:	I'm not going to tell you that, but you should know that they're concerned about you. The purpose of our talk today is not to tell you of any conclusions I've reached about you, but to make it clear that I can't tolerate any confusion regarding the decisions I make. Any employee on the team has to support the decisions that are made. If you or anyone else feels unable to do that, then the option is to leave the company. I certainly don't want you to do that because I value you and your contribution. But my experience has taught me that an undercurrent that works against management's decisions is a poison that can really damage an organization. I don't mean to sound judgmental or hard, but I do want to be very clear about this. Before a decision on anything is made, I want all the advice and opposing suggestions that people have to offer. But once things are in motion, I expect every employee to support the direction we're taking. Do I make myself clear?
Employee:	So what are you saying? Would you fire me?
Manager:	I realize we're speaking hypothetically here, but I would have little choice. There is no one in this organization who wouldn't be replaced if he or she was behaving in an insubordinate way. No one is bigger than the team. And no one who acts contrary to management direction, or gets others to think that they can act against management, should think that he is immune from termination.
Employee:	Well, that's clear enough, I guess, but it seems to me that what you're really doing is putting me in my place and telling me to shut my mouth.
Manager:	No, you're wrong. Anytime you think I'm out of line, I want you to come to me and tell me to my face. You're welcome in here anytime, and frankly, I need to be told when I make mistakes. I won't react

	negatively to that. The only thing I do ask is that folks be straight with me. Tell me to my face, but with the others, keep your opinions to yourself and stick to doing the job you're paid to do. Is that fair?
Employee:	Yes, I can live with that. I don't think you're always right, and if you're willing to give me a hearing, there won't be any undercutting to the others.
Manager:	Thank you, Harriet. I really respect that, and I'm glad we had the chance to clear the air. I feel good about the way you've discussed this with me today.

In this feedback session, it's important that the manager overtly express displeasure over whatever is bothering him. It's permissible, even effective, to raise your voice a little (without becoming abusive) or even to slam your fist on the table if such behavior is normal for you. Let the employee see that you're agitated or really upset if you are. It's dishonest to an employee to hide your emotion or to pretend that you're such a rational human being that you never have any feelings. If you will show the employee your anger, your frustration, your worry, and tell him straight out how the problem affects you and how it's affecting other people, I think that lets the employee see this exchange as something more than an intellectual exercise. But remember this important rule: When you express displeasure, you must also express a feeling of confidence in the employee.

> You know, I really don't understand why you're letting yourself get off track, Mary. I've been so pleased with everything else you've done that I can't imagine why you're now letting yourself down, letting your co-workers down. That's just not you. I know you can do better than that.

So I think there's a balanced picture that you must present, involving not only positive and negative information but positive and negative emotion.

One last suggestion in terms of these employee-counseling sessions: I wouldn't make them extremely confrontational, and I wouldn't make them overly long. I'd keep them fairly short and to the point, and let this become part of your normal supervisory communication style. Basically, they are word-to-the-wise sessions. Just a word should do the trick. "To the wise" implies that if they're smart enough, your problem employees will clean up their act on their own. All they need, if they're really good people, aware people, is that succinct, candid message. They'll get with the program if they know where they now stand with you. Admit it. Wasn't there ever a time in your life when a parent, boss, or friend pulled you up short and set you straight?

3. Document! Document! Document!

The third step in the positive-discipline sequence is to start documenting like crazy. If the initial counseling sessions in the second step have not paid off, if the employee has not responded, then it's very clear that his behavior is not just a temporary deviation. This is a person who is not on track, and is not wise enough to get with the program once you've pointed out his deficiencies. At this stage, you have to face the unpleasant prospect that this case may eventually require some very strong medicine, perhaps a termination. And that, in turn, could even lead to a lawsuit. This is why it's so important that you start to document — for example, by keeping records and by dictating reports of how your conferences went. Because of my belief that people respond best to honesty, I would let the employee know that this information is being kept:

> I've talked with you, Dan, in several sessions now, about the quality of your work. I've told you exactly how I feel, and you know, I just don't think you're getting with it. As part of the normal process in these cases, I'm now starting to keep a record of your performance. I'm going to have to spend some of my time to keep track of this thing. Isn't this sad? Since I believe in letting people know where they stand, I wanted you to know that I'm keeping this record.

Now, advising the employee is going to have several effects. First, it communicates to Dan that you're serious. It also communicates to Dan that if disciplinary action follows at some future point, he might want to react then in some other way than by getting angry. You see, one of the things Dan knows is that you've got a big fat file on him. I think that has a positive psychological effect — it lets the employee know that you probably have solid evidence about his performance and that you're not going to be fooled at some later time. The benefit of this is that it helps Dan to grasp the fact that things are becoming serious. It also lets him know that you're preparing for further action. This may jar Dan into getting his performance back on track. If it doesn't, it still provides a base for you to stand on when stricter measures must be taken.

In that file you are to put facts only. Just like Joe Friday used to say on *Dragnet,* "The facts, ma'am, nothing but the facts." Avoid writing down opinions, or conjecture, or hearsay. What we are interested in is what you know, what you saw, what others report based on their direct observation. Don't state in the record that you think he's having a midlife crisis or she must be menopausal. Stay away from such subjective and potentially ignorant comments. Instead, simply report the facts of the employee's behavior — what it is that the employee has or has not done. In the event that your handling of the situation later becomes a basis for legal action, don't let your own words be a source of embarrassment to you in court.

Sometimes the question arises as to whose records these are. Occasionally, an employee will want to see "his" record. Generally, the courts have ruled that these are not the employee's records, but the employer's. However, there is no guarantee that any particular judge would hold to that view, especially in these days of full disclosure and freedom-of-information thinking. So while this is the employer's record of dealings with an employee, it is always good judgment to enter into that record facts only. The record will never embarrass you if it's founded on solid evidence.

4. Review the Situation

The next step in positive discipline is to perform a complete review of the situation. At this point, you have assessed what is wrong with the employee's performance, calculated its cost to you, and had some initial, and apparently unsuccessful, employee-counseling sessions. And most recently, you have opened a file and compiled relevant documentation. Now it's time to sit down and consider the entire case.

It is at this juncture that your organization's discipline policy needs to be reviewed and thoroughly understood. Nearly all organizations of any size have specific discipline policies, which may cover a step-by-step sequence of verbal and written warnings, rights of appeal, and other related matters.

Generally speaking, I don't like discipline policies that become quasi-legal, nor do I like those that become overly detailed or complicated. I think it sends the wrong kinds of messages. I also don't care for policies that provide for layoffs or other types of punishment. I just don't like dealing with people on that level, and I don't like having a working relationship that is fundamentally negative. But at the same time, I am in favor of whatever works best for you, so I wouldn't want to flatly state that all discipline policies should follow a single standard model. There is enough variation between industries and groups of employees that "whatever works" has to be the rule of thumb.

If you're in a very small organization, it's possible that there may be no written discipline policy. My suggestion is that you use the specific case you're working on now to create at least the beginnings of such a policy. Write down exactly the steps you feel are fair and that you've gone through, and use that as the first draft of a policy statement, which may be expanded later. Then have that statement reviewed by your legal counsel.

The purpose of policy is to give you a clear road map or at least establish some general guidelines. Disciplinary situations sometimes get emotional and complicated. Management must agree on a uniform series of steps that are to be taken. In part, policy helps guide decision making, and in part, it represents evidence of due process that would be important in building a legal case should that become necessary.

The courts have generally ruled that a policy that is not enforced is a nonpolicy and that the practices that are followed become the de facto (actual) policy. Let me restate that: In the event you have a written policy that specifies a certain way of handling given situations, but you don't handle things that way and make all kinds of excuses and allow all kinds of exceptions and deviations from that policy, it is the pattern of those deviations from policy that will generally be ruled by the court to be the true policy followed by your organization. For this reason, it becomes very important that management strictly enforce the policy in order to protect the organization.

After reviewing the discipline policy, a full discussion with human resources management is called for. At this time, you're ready for a review of the specifics of the case, and it is often helpful to sit down with someone more experienced, go through the situation step by step, and let that person test whether you have done what needs to be done in disciplinary cases.

Another element of the situation review is to develop your action plan. What are you going to do next with Tom or Mary? What would be the first thing you would do? The second? When will you do it? What kinds of support elements will need to be in place? And so on.

At this point, you have thoroughly reviewed the situation. And now the time has come to act, and act expeditiously. If you need to do a bit of housecleaning in terms of straightening some people out about your expectations or dealing with them in a helpful, supportive way so they can shape up their performance, then do it now. It is important that you act quickly, so the poor behavior does not keep poisoning your work unit. Thus, the situation review is not designed to slow you down, but rather is a final check before you proceed to take direct action.

5. Implement Your Action Agenda

The next step in the positive-discipline process is to implement whatever action you've decided on. In no particular order of priority, here are some corrective measures that might be included in an action agenda:

1. *Education and training.* Under this approach, there might be some special on-the-job training or some specific coaching from you, or you might pair this person under a buddy system with an effective worker who could serve as a role model. Education and training are an appropriate course of action when you determine that the person does not know how to do the task, or there's some question about the person's knowledge of how to perform the task, or the person hasn't performed the task in some time.

However, education and training are not a reasonable course of action when you're dealing primarily with a motivational or attitudinal problem. One of the most common errors that managers make in taking action is to send people off to a training program when there is in fact a need to deal with an attitudinal, motivational, or personality problem.

2. *Supervisory counseling.* Sometimes the manager is the counseling source the person comes to. Just by listening and talking and "being there" for others, the manager can help some people deal with their problems.

3. *Psychological counseling.* The manager has to be able to identify those cases that he can't handle. If simple, friendly talk doesn't help, professional advice is in order. Referring the person either to an in-house specialist or to an outside community resource may be the best course of action.

4. *Employee assistance program (EAP).* These programs have become increasingly popular in recent years. A number of companies have started to group specific programs such as health promotion, counseling, benefits planning, and others into an overall employee assistance program. If your organization has an EAP, you might discuss your current problem case with the program's administrator. Together you can assess the employee's needs and the organization's resources, then plan a coordinated approach to problem solving.

5. *Warnings.* Another tactic might be to issue specific warnings. Under some discipline policies, a set number of warnings, either verbal or in writing, are given, usually following the rule of "three times and out." In issuing a warning, management takes the view that there's nothing it can do to solve the employee's problem. The employee is going to have to solve his own problem. Meanwhile, management is making it abundantly clear that it's not going to tolerate this performance past a certain point and that the employee is now on thin ice.

6. *Social censure.* Another avenue for action might be social censure. In some cases, the work group does this for you by not inviting the offending party to social events,

lunch, an after-work get-together, and so on. Sometimes a supervisor might censure a subordinate socially by not smiling at the person, or by frowning, even though the supervisor might smile at everyone in the group (except Tom), slap everybody on the back (except Tom), chuckle and joke and speak with everybody in the unit (except Tom), invite everybody to the house for the Christmas party (except Tom). The decision to employ social censure is certainly a personal values question, and some supervisors won't be comfortable with this approach, but it is a powerful, forceful way of getting the message across. I think the real question is, how well do you know your people? It was said of Vince Lombardi that one of the reasons he was so successful was that he knew whom to pat on the back and whom to kick in the pants, dealing with each member of his team in a way that worked for that particular individual. While I certainly cringe to think of being on the receiving end of that kind of approach, I've seen it work — and work very successfully, in certain cases.

7. *Reducing rewards.* Another item on the action agenda might be to reduce rewards. I said previously that I don't like layoffs, which in essence reduce a person's take-home pay for the days not worked. The reason I dislike layoffs is that this approach says to the problem employee that the only way we can solve your performance problem *on* the job is to send you *off* the job. I think that inviting people to leave the premises isn't really dealing with their central need to adapt better at work. I guess I'd rather have them on the job and working on their problem than home watching television and being rewarded with entertainment.

But there are more productive ways in which rewards can be manipulated to influence employee performance — for example, holding up merit increases, or reducing other financial or nonfinancial rewards. It's precisely here that I make my case against cost-of-living adjustments. I've seen all kinds of cases where a manager is struggling with a poorly performing employee, and in the middle of this process, the employee gets his cost-of-living adjustment! The organization has just rewarded the employee at the same time that he is performing inappropriately. This sends people a confusing message: They don't understand why you would continue to increase their salary if they're really that bad. I think that pay should be for performance only, and when you don't perform, you don't get pay increases.

Don't confuse the issue in people's minds by providing pay for reasons other than merit or incentive. Some organizations think the choice at review time should be between getting a salary increase and getting no increase. But another viewpoint is that salary review time is a chance to determine whether you get a salary increase or a salary decrease. I agree with this latter approach: The options should be that you could get more or you could get less! That may seem a little extreme, but I would submit that some people are worth less than they were a year ago and that to continue to reward them at the level of their former performance is overpayment.

A modification of that position is to have the job regraded, classifying it downward, based on the person's not performing tasks at a higher level. People generally react very strongly to tampering with the reward structure — which indicates its strength as a possible tactic. As a matter of practicality, most managers will simply approve the annual merit increase, finding that to be the easiest course of action, but doing so sends a signal that one can get away with coasting in this organization and thereby reinforces the unwanted behavior.

8. *Punishment.* There are those who would consider punishing people to be another item on the action agenda. But punishment is contrary to this book's main point: We're trying to positively discipline people rather than punish them. The major problem behavior modification specialists report with punishment is that its effect is not very predictable. That is, a person who is punished may simply rebel, as opposed to changing his behavior. It's uncertain what type of response you'll get. The goal here is not a fight but a change of behavior. Yet some organizations will inflict certain punishments. Sometimes individual managers will give the problem person a series of disagreeable assignments or try to maneuver the person out of the organization by increasing his or her job dissatisfaction.

One manager in a civil service organization reported that it was so difficult to get people out of his system that he had to find creative ways to sandbag them. In one instance, he set up a subordinate to give a presentation in front of the next six higher levels of management. The young man blew his presentation so badly that it subsequently became much easier for him to be removed from the organization as a result. It seems to me that such an approach isn't very humane or ethical, but it is a course of action taken by some managers.

9. *Supervisory support.* Often the manager's action agenda is to provide continuing support by way of communication, taking the person under his wing, and providing a high level of consideration and caring in the relationship. I recall vividly the events of 1964 and early 1965. At one conference in the grand ballroom of the Waldorf Astoria, personnel executives from all over the United States had gathered to discuss the potential impact of the 1964 civil rights legislation. Under its provisions, certain groups that had been discriminated against in the past on the grounds of race, religion, and other factors were now to be admitted to the workforce. The general concern among the personnel executives there, in all honesty, was what's going to happen to our organizations? Are we going to see a decline in our employees' capability, coupled with a decline in organizational performance, as we hire a bunch of people who lack the necessary skills, people whom we've screened out in the past?

To a very large extent, the problems that people predicted in those days never became a reality in American business organizations. There were many explanations for this, of course. In some cases, for instance, the newly hired employees possessed a lot more skill and expertise than they had been given credit for. But I think one of the great stories of American management (which has never been told anywhere else, as far as I'm aware) is the fact that a lot of people *were* hired who lacked the necessary job skills, were below adequate literacy levels, and had low levels of self-confidence — and yet they succeeded. Why? These people entered a working world where a bunch of high-achievement supervisors, including some who may not have wanted these new workers hired, basically made the commitment that they were not going to fail. Whether the supervisors were dedicated to equal employment opportunity was immaterial. They were men and women of achievement who were determined that their unit operations were not going to suffer. And some of these supervisors, motivated in certain cases by a desire to serve humanity and motivated in other cases merely by a desire to comply with the law, took these newcomers under their wing and supported them and gave them the impetus to go forward and to achieve.

Often, the good supervisor or co-worker who is sensitive to the needs of the troubled person and helps him or her meet those needs can take a performance deficiency and turn it into a performance strength. The generation of American managers in the sixties and seventies who took personal responsibility and would not let people fail in their work performance even though they may have failed in every other arena they were previously involved in deserves credit for a remarkable achievement. And so I think providing supportive help and making a commitment to the person in difficulty are powerful and appropriate actions that can be taken.

There may be other action agendas that can be pursued. I think you have to use some creativity in designing your agenda on a case-by-case basis. There is no single path, no magic way, and managers have to devise strategies that will work with each individual.

6. Monitor for Compliance

Once the action agenda has been decided on and implemented, then it's important to monitor the problem employee's progress (or lack of it) on an ongoing basis. Generally, the person is in sufficient difficulty at this point that daily or weekly reviews of his or her performance are called for. I really can't see reviewing performance on a monthly basis. Sometimes you'll see employees who get called into the office and receive a warning, but then the boss doesn't follow up and check where they stand in the coming 30-day period. I don't believe benign neglect solves the problem. I think that part of the action agenda, or certainly an outgrowth of the action agenda, has to be compliance monitoring. How is the employee doing day by day and week by week?

An active inspection is what is called for at this time. Among the things it accomplishes are maintaining a certain psychological pressure and establishing closeness of the supervisor to the supervised. This watchful atmosphere helps the person stay within very narrow bounds, in full knowledge that you are right there on top of the situation; it reinforces your earlier verbal messages.

The employee may now respond favorably to your action agenda. He gets it together, and that's the end of the problem. But there's the other possibility — yet another failure. At this point, you have to decide how many more chances you want to give this person. Often you have to recycle the process, going back to the action agenda, repeating potentially effective tactics, and then monitoring, trying different things. I think there is a virtue in testing different approaches. But there comes a time when I would suggest that you've got to start facing up to some hard realities — namely, the action agendas that you've been able to devise, can afford, or are in the range of what you are willing to undertake may be insufficient to accomplish the desired result. How many times you want to return to the action list and try different approaches is strictly a judgment call. Some managers are inclined to give problem employees one or two chances only; other managers may be willing to give them two or three or even considerably more. My own judgment is that, in most cases, if your efforts haven't succeeded after three attempts, they're not going to succeed at all.

7. Issue a Final Warning

That brings us to the final warning. Under most discipline policies, a final warning is called for. This is the point in the relationship with the employee at which he gets an ultimatum. This individual must now either turn his performance around or be shown the door. Substantially more will be said about final warnings in Chapter 11. I'll introduce you then to a seven-step process known as power counseling that can be effective in saving a remarkable number of people at this late stage.

The bare bones of the final warning are an announcement, usually verbal, that spells out what behavior has to change by what date, and what the consequences will be if it doesn't change. Because this is the final warning, the consequence being spoken of is nearly always termination. Generally, this is not a discussion, although some discussion could be appropriate. Certainly, it is not a time for management to equivocate. This is not a negotiation session, but rather a warning that the employee is teetering on the brink. If the situation does not call for the power-counseling approach as a last-ditch effort to save the employee, then this final-warning announcement is the minimum action required to back management up if legal proceedings subsequently result.

One other point to keep in mind is that certain offenses do not warrant a final warning or even preliminary warnings. These are acts so serious or grievous that they require immediate termination. These differ from place to place, based on the judgment of management, but may include:

Theft
Gross insubordination
Use of alcohol or drugs on the job
Knowingly engaging in unsafe practices
Sabotage of company operations

8. Proceed with Termination/Resignation

If the final-warning discussion does not work, then the last step in the positive discipline of problem employees is to proceed with termination or give them the opportunity to resign. Even termination can be handled in a positive way, and I'll provide some specific guidance for how to deal with that in Chapter 12.

Summary

The positive discipline of problem employees, then, is an eight-step sequence. First, analyze the performance deficiency and its cost to you. Second, provide initial employee-counseling sessions that give people feedback regarding their performance. Third, maintain extensive documentation to prepare you in the event of further, more serious, action. Fourth, do a complete review of the situation in order to create the fifth step, an agenda of specific actions that you're going to take with this person. Sixth, monitor that agenda for compliance. The seventh step is to have the final-warning conversation. Step eight is the termination/resignation process.

Our goal is discipleship, not punishment. Since we're after satisfactory performance, winning behavior, we need not feel uncomfortable or emotionally overinvolved about moving through a series of increasingly serious measures.

8

Making Communication Work

Managers routinely report that it seems impossible to get through to problem employees. One frustrated manager said to me in a recent conference, "I've told him a hundred times, and he just doesn't seem to hear, or even want to hear." How can you reach these people?

Normally, we learn from our experiences. When people frown at us for inappropriate behavior, they communicate that they think we ought to change, and we tend to avoid that behavior in future. When people smile at us in appreciation for something we've done, we tend to repeat that behavior. In short, we learn how to behave, and learn how to modify present behavior, largely through the feedback we receive from others.

The capability of the human mind to redirect behavior based on external feedback pays off for us in our approaches to boss, workmates, and life situations in general. While problem employees also receive these feedback signals, messages, and vibes, they are perceptually deficient. They either do not understand the implications of these feedback signals or somehow block out their meaning.

Does Counseling Work?

This brings us to an interesting debate: Are the same kinds of counseling approaches that are part of normal communication really appropriate for the problem person? The whole idea that we can change behavior by simply providing more feedback is based on the assumption that the people being counseled want to change or are capable of change if only they had adequate information. But if problem employees have communication and perceptual problems that are beyond the ability of most managers to handle, maybe communication should be dismissed as a strategy for dealing with these people. After all, busy managers are not versed in psychotherapeutic approaches or advanced counseling techniques. So just what is realistic to expect of both manager and problem employee?

A number of studies suggest that the supervisor has a better chance of changing behavior by arranging consequences — for example, loss of pay, time off from work, or threat of termination. By spelling out the consequences rather than relying on communication methods, the supervisor is more likely to reach the problem worker. It's amazing how certain types of messages do get through!

My own belief, based on the evidence, is that the latter approach is probably more likely to do the trick than giving the culprit a "talking to." Certainly, the effectiveness of a behavior-modifying approach, arranging positive or negative consequences, seems to be confirmed by the experience of working managers. Their understandable exasperation in dealing with problem people usually kills their interest in sitting down to have yet another chat. If one listens to what managers say, one finds they would rather take action than provide counseling, especially after they've had some previous verbal jousts.

Nonetheless, this not to say there is no value in counseling techniques, and certainly an understanding of some of the major principles underlying human communication may be helpful. A review of the essentials will give the manager an opportunity to check his own approach to the person. For those managers who have lost faith in communication principles as they apply to problem people, let me assure you that even though communication methods have only a limited ability to change behavior, they have great power to assist you in eliciting information that can help you diagnose the problem. Gaining some meaningful insights can enable you to decide with greater confidence just what you're going to do with this person.

The Connected Communicator

One of the most firmly established principles of counseling and psychotherapy is that counseling technique is secondary to a perception on the part of the person being counseled that the therapist is genuinely interested and wants to help. In counseling, what matters most is the extent of our ability to make a conection with the person. As a practical matter, quit trying to figure out what's going on in the other person's head, and don't worry about assigning psychological labels. What matters is that the other person feels a connection to you.

A second general pattern found in cases where a therapist was able to get through to patients was that the patients described the therapist as empathetic, understanding, and trustworthy. If the patients believed the therapist was working in their best interest and trusted the therapist, the patients were then able to utilize the skills of their trained professional helper to achieve better life adjustments.

What all this means is that whether trained as a therapist or not, any person who is perceived by a troubled party as having that party's best interests at heart and is trusted by him has a much higher probability of actually being helpful. That means that a spouse, a good friend, a pastor, a boss, anyone who is able to establish a connection with the person needing help can often be of assistance.

The only caveat that should be noted is that when the problem employee is truly emotionally disturbed, a well-meaning and helpful manager is going to be out of his depth. But saying that an interested and caring supervisor can, in certain cases, be as effective in getting through as a psychotherapist is not to disparage the professional. In fact, the ability of the psychotherapist to deal with serious or deep-rooted problems, as well as with mental pathology, comes from specialized training. On the other hand, supervisors need not feel that they must be a psychologist to be able to get problem employees to want to reach out for a better adjustment in their lives.

What this means for the practicing manager is that if the relationship you now have with the problem person is full of animosity and lack of trust and has deteriorated, it is highly unlikely that counseling is going to be successful. But it also means that if the employee is able to perceive that you do care, and there is a bond between you, then there is some possibility that that employee may be able to cross that bridge back to you and to better behavior. If that bond is there, or if it can be created, then counseling may be a useful approach to salvaging this person.

What's Your Communication Stance?

A great deal has been written in recent years about the need to be assertive. Assertiveness is basically a communication stance in which individuals have their say, speak honestly and forthrightly, without blaming or denigrating others. Some managers are so uncertain about how to handle problem employees that they largely do nothing and let the situation drift. This is a passive response to a situation that calls for action, and the supervisor's passivity is seen in his not providing feedback, not smiling, avoiding the employee, or talking about the employee to others.

Maturity in management is seen when the manager deals with the problem situation in a businesslike fashion. You have a perfect right to speak up and to help the troubled person understand the situation as it is. To fail to speak up in a positive way is a dereliction of duty.

At the other end of the scale is the aggressive supervisor who, with hostility and anger, berates employees repeatedly, attributes all kinds of negative motivations and beliefs to them, rips them apart, tears them down, chews them up, and spits them out. The hostile supervisor is overreacting, perhaps out of his own insecurities or even because of a need for power. Power in management is not the ability to yell at somebody and get away with it. True power is the ability to get results through people by dealing with them respectfully. Like passivity, aggressiveness is not going to be very helpful in establishing the kind of supportive relationship and effective feedback that will help problem employees change. It only drives them further away and gives them a justification for continuing their inappropriate behavior.

And so, assertive confrontation is neither passive nor aggressive. It is open, honest, forthright, and to the point. It operates out of respect for the other person and a belief that the other may want to take some action. It both protects a manager's self-esteem and provides an arena in which the employee has some chance for improvement. So be assertive and direct in your communications. You have nothing to apologize for, nothing to be afraid of.

The Communication Paradigm

When one examines a model of communications, it includes a message sender who encodes his or her message through various means and then transmits that message to a message receiver. In turn, each receiver becomes a sender, and it is this cycling back and forth of information that creates communication.

But communication is more than just the sending and receiving of messages. Communication has at its root the word *unity*. To have communion or community or communication is to have co-unity, oneness with the other. Problems in communication arise because of barriers that impede the ability of the sender to get his or her message through to the receiver. Barriers are of three types: those that are internal to the sender, those that are in the situational environment between the sender and the receiver, and those that are within the receiver. Understanding the nature of these barriers is useful to the supervisor in terms of enabling him to determine what needs to be done in order to successfully communicate with unresponsive people. Let's start by taking a look at the barriers that exist within the supervisor.

The Supervisor's Internal Barriers

There are eight major barriers to communication that can affect the manager's ability to get his or her own message out:

1. *Lack of confidence.* Managers simply do not use problem employee counseling skills on a frequent basis and therefore are unsure of themselves. This causes them to be preoccupied with how they are conducting the counseling session rather than focused on the person and his problem.

2. *Bias and prejudice.* We all are victims of our own views of the world. Bias and prejudice need not be powerfully negative and obvious forces; they can be only subconscious and subtly influencing. One of the most common difficulties that a manager has to deal with in confronting a problem employee is the manager's own internalized values about achievement, the need to do things correctly and with excellence, and so on. The fact is that many people do not necessarily view the work arena with the same kind of dedication that a good manager has. And within certain bounds, it doesn't make sense for a manager to look askance at people who are not guided by the same values at work as he is.

3. *Perceptual set.* You can't tell a book by its cover, but many managers insist on trying to do so when it comes to people. A classic story, possibly apocryphal, describes a speech by General Electric's vice-president of human resources. Addressing a large audience of GE's college recruiters, he asked these interviewers what they would think of inviting a certain peculiar candidate to Schenectady, the headquarters of GE:

> What would be your reaction to inviting in a candidate who wore a rumpled and dirty suit that looked as if he'd slept in it, whose long hair and unkempt beard indicated that he took little interest in personal grooming, who chewed tobacco and whose clothing bore the stains of tobacco juice, who had the physical disability of a hunched back, causing him to limp as he walked, who spoke English very poorly, and who tended to be very brusque and rude to people? How many of you would be willing to invite into the home office such a one and stake your reputation on this person's capabilities? [Not a hand in the audience went up.]

> Ladies and gentlemen, I have just described to you Charles Proteus Steinmetz, without whom there would be no General Electric.

We tend to judge by the surface cues that people present rather than looking deeper. When we're dealing with a problem employee, we sometimes lose sight of the wholeness of this human being and deal only with his most readily visible problem.

4. *Impulsiveness and premature judgment.* When we like people and approve of them, we tend to think positively of nearly everything that they do. In like fashion, if we have a bad impression of people, we tend to judge negatively everything that they do. This is sometimes called the "halo or horns" effect. We see them at one extreme or the other—wearing either a halo or horns.

5. *Poor counseling skills.* It's not uncommon for managers to be unable to effectively use counseling techniques. They ask the wrong questions, don't listen carefully, or become defensive during the communication process. They contribute to poor communications.

6. *Failure to listen with the "third ear."* I've formulated two rules for communication:

> Whatever I say it is, it isn't.
> Whatever I say it is, there is always more.

People *never* tell you the whole story. They tell you part of the story. Thus, "Whatever I say it is, there is always more." In like fashion, if we're reluctant to reveal the truth of a situation, we sometimes give surface reasons but not the underlying explanation. Thus, "Whatever I say it is, it isn't." We are so clever that we manage to speak in ways that don't communicate!

One clue to whether other people have more to say is to look at their body language. Does the way they carry themselves say they're tense, open, relaxed, edgy? To what degree do they make eye contact? And so forth. While the ability to listen to what a person says is certainly important, the ability to listen to a person with the "third ear" —to listen between the words, to hear messages that aren't even spoken—is also a critical skill area.

7. *Failure to recognize the "arc of distortion."* The arc of distortion is a label that has been pinned on the normal distortion effects that occur with language. This phenomenon is nicely captured in the following popular saying:

> I know you believe you understand what you thought I said, but I'm not sure you realize that what you heard is not what I meant!

Because supervisors are generally good with language skills, they often don't see the limits of those skills.

8. *Distracting behaviors.* Managers themselves are sometimes a source of distracting behavior. Some managers, without realizing it, will frown, tap their pencil nervously, send facial signals that say to the other person: "I don't believe you. I don't have time for you. I don't want to hear this." The inability to listen openly and nonjudgmentally creates a barrier to the communication process.

Barriers in the Environment

Controlling communication barriers within ourselves is probably more difficult than controlling those in the external environment. Therefore, a cardinal rule in communications management is to minimize environmental interruptions and work to overcome factors that can hamper understanding. These include:

1. *Background noise and "fishbowl" communication.* The counseling discussion should always take place in a closed office with telephone messages held and other disruptions prevented. If there are windows or clear partitions between offices, the participants should face away from them so that other people cannot see facial expressions and so that outside movements will not distract those working on a problem.

2. *Belief in the mechanistic communication fallacy.* Managers who say, "I've told this guy a hundred times," assume that the person is deliberately disobeying. The fact is that words said are not necessarily words received. How you send a message to another person, and your selection of words, become very important.

Did you know that the 500 most commonly used words in the English language have a total of 20,000 different dictionary meanings? That means that every time you use one of these words, the other person has to pick out the one meaning that you intended from the 400 meanings, on average, that it has!

3. *Use of emotionally charged or incomprehensible language.* Language, as the mechanism by which we send our communication arrow toward the other person's target, has words that create emotional responses, such as profanity, racial labels, chauvinistic expressions, and the like. The other problem is that even if we can avoid using words that deliberately provoke negative reactions, we're faced with the fact that other people may simply have vocabulary limitations. Managers typically have more education than their employees. They use more advanced language, have more sophisticated operating concepts about the business, and so forth. When they communicate using words and concepts that are commonly understood among their management peers, they may be choosing terminology that is simply not going to be understood by the employee.

I believe the greatest enemy of communications is the illusion of it. We live in a world in which we're continually inundated with messages and in which thousands of words per hour are flung around. To think that all of this is somehow resulting in meaningful communication is a mistake. Marriage counselors report that it's not uncommon for people who have lived together for years, with feelings of regard and love and concern for each other, to have communication problems. If people who have really worked at this process over a long period of time have difficulty, how can we possibly expect that people at work are automatically going to understand us clearly and effectively?

All of these findings simply suggest that we should confine ourselves to common, everyday words, speak simply, speak as we would be spoken to. Keep messages short; keep asking for feedback: "Did you understand what I said? Do you have any questions about what I've said? Would you please paraphrase or repeat what I've said?" And keep working at it. If you've already told them a hundred times, then it simply means that you now have to tell them for the hundred and first time.

Barriers in the Employee

Not only do barriers exist in the manager and in the communication environment; they also exist in the employee, and these latter barriers are perhaps the most important of all:

1. *Emotional factors.* Employees report feelings of anxiety, fear, and insecurity in counseling situations. They often exhibit low self-confidence, many of them all too painfully aware that they are not meeting expectations. That kind of emotional state is hardly conducive to their engaging in a meaningful dialog.

2. *Power differential.* Employees are in a situation where they're dealing with an authority figure and where they perceive their own power and authority as being very limited. No matter how you look at it, it is the boss who has the power. Even in a situation where the employee is a union member, his or her power relationship with the supervisor is an uncertain one.

3. *Lack of candor.* Like everyone else, employees have been conditioned to conceal their true feelings and attitudes. They live behind a mask.

4. *Receptivity.* Employees's ability to communicate can also be limited by their endurance. Because of fatigue, it's more difficult for them to discuss things after working a ten-hour shift. So if you can talk with employees when they're fresh and better able to receive your message, it may help.

While the manager can eliminate or reduce some of the communication barriers, particularly those in the environment and in himself, there's a limit to what the manager can accomplish in terms of a barrier-reduction strategy.

A second and better strategy can be tried: *Set up the situation so the employee comes across the barriers to you.* Let the employee do the work of getting through the barriers. It is precisely with this approach that the use of good questioning and listening skills becomes important. In essence, a question is an invitation — an invitation for the employee to overcome the barriers in order to reach the manager.

Questioning and Listening Techniques

There are several key objectives in counseling problem people. Since problem employees are often emotionally troubled, supervisors should allow them to verbalize and talk out their problems, thus giving them the opportunity to *air their concerns.* In this particular situation, the goal of the supervisors is to do a minimum of talking while the employees talk 80 percent to 90 percent of the time.

Second, supervisors want to enhance their own understanding of the factors affecting the employee's performance and the explanations that the employees give for that performance. For that reason, supervisors will want to use this counseling session as an opportunity to sharpen their *diagnosis* of what's going on.

For both reasons — airing concerns and diagnosis — supervisors need to use their questioning and listening skills. And the simple strategy is to get employees to come through the communication barriers to the supervisors. This can best be accomplished by facilitating the communication process, or smoothing the communication pathway, for employees. To ask questions is to send an "I want to know" signal. To ask questions and listen for responses is to draw employees in, making them feel less distant. To question and listen is to indicate acceptance of the employees as people, even if the managers reject their behavior. Let's quickly review the seven major questioning and listening techniques.

Questioning: Running the Funnel

A very useful format for employing questioning skills is to run the funnel. Running the funnel means to start with questions that are very broad and open, very nondirective, and gradually narrow those questions down to specifics. We begin at the top of the funnel and end up at the bottom. The process of running the funnel involves four types of questions:

1. *Broad information-gathering questions.* A suggested technique is to start each counseling session with the question, "Tell me about _____." The phrase "tell me about" is both an invitation and a command.

> Tell me about why you're late this morning.
> Tell me about the situation between you and Mary.
> Tell me about what's been going on with you lately.

This sort of question is so broad that the employee can go in any direction and tell you about any piece of the puzzle. The supervisor should listen carefully because how the employee decides to start telling the story can shed considerable light on his thought processes.

In a sense, the manager is saying to the person, "Paint me a picture." Just as a painter could start either with trees and clouds or with some of the human figures in the foreground, so it is in a manager-employee counseling session: Some employees will go directly to a discussion of the figures in the foreground, while others will tend to talk about the bushes at the edge of the scene. Those who start on the periphery are not to be criticized; it's simply an indication that they are unable, at least immediately, to deal with some of the more central themes or substantive elements of the picture.

While "Tell me about _____" is an invitation, that invitation also has a directive tone to it that signals: "I expect to hear the answer to this question. I want you to fill me in on what's happening." "Tell me about" is the top of the funnel, the broadest area, the discussion opener that grants the employee the greatest degree of room to roam.

2. *Open-ended questions.* The basic interrogative, or question, words in the English language are *what, where, why, when, how,* and *who.* This poem by Rudyard Kipling says it all:

> I keep six honest serving men
> (They taught me all I knew);
> Their names are What and Why and When
> And How and Where and Who.

The best way to learn is to ask a question. The six honest serving men will teach the supervisor most of what he needs to know about any problem situation. As the employee paints the picture of what's going on, the supervisor can direct the employee to fill in different areas of the canvas. "What happened then? Who else was involved? When did this occur? Where were you at the time?" All these are open-ended questions.

A close-ended question is one that can be answered with a simple yes or no. The problem with close-ended questions is that they don't prompt the subordinate to offer any additional information and the supervisor may have to lead the employee question by question. "Have you been coming in late every day? Do you intend to correct this behavior? Am I going to have to discipline you?" Another problem with close-ended questions is that they can elicit terribly misleading information. No matter how you answer "Have you stopped selling drugs yet?" you lose! Open-ended questions cannot be answered with a simple yes or no. They have to be answered with some description.

Notice that *what, where, why, when, how,* and *who* are more directive than the simple invitation, "Tell me about _____." They are more focused, not as broad. As a consequence, the supervisor must ask a whole stream of the "*w*'s and *h*" questions in order to get a fair amount of information. While it takes only a few seconds to ask such questions, it requires far more time to answer them. In this series of questions, the employee, with the supervisor's assistance, completes the outline of the painting.

3. *Detailed, specific questions.* These questions go after fine points that may not have been made entirely clear by the basic inquiries. They may include some yes/no questions and in other ways elicit additional detailed information. "Did this happen before or after Joe pushed you? Were you here at 8:15 or 8:25?"

Notice how far down the funnel the questioning has come and how extremely specific the questions have become. In addition to being at the bottom of the funnel, we are also at the point of having the picture fully sketched in, but the picture is still only in black and white. To gain the color, we need our fourth type of question.

4. *Self-evaluation questions.* Emotion is the color of life. When we're mad, we see red; when we're depressed, we are blue; when we feel energetic, the color is green for go. By running the funnel, the picture has been painted. Now the manager needs to ask some questions about how the person evaluates the situation that he's described: "As you see it, Fred, what does all this mean?" Or, "How did you feel when Grenelda said that to you?" At this point, the employee's description of his mood, feelings, and emotional reactions will provide a very helpful clue. It is here that the color is added to the picture.

Note that the emotional questions can only be addressed *after* the funnel has been run. That is, once the manager has taken the time to listen to the employee, the employee feels more open in his responses. A bond of trust has been established. Now, when the supervisor asks for an emotional rating or a subjective description of the experience, the employee feels inclined to trust the supervisor with that information. On the other hand, if the supervisor had started the conversation by asking about the employee's emotional state, the employee would likely have clammed up.

Listening: Greasing the Slide

While the levels of questioning represent a funneling process, or a process comparable to that of painting a picture, listening skills can best be likened to a process of greasing the slide. Listening responses are utilized as appropriate during the running of the funnel. These do not occur in any order but are comprised of three types:

1. *Restating and rephrasing.* This technique is sometimes called mirror listening. You take what you've heard, rephrase it, and say it back to the person.

Let me see if I've got this straight . . .
In other words, you felt that this was the way it happened.
It wasn't the money so much as the lack of being recognized for the work you did that got you upset.

When you echo the employee, what you're doing is holding up a version of the picture he has painted, or a portion of that picture, and saying: "This is what I've received as you were sending me the message. Do I have this picture correct?" The other person can then respond by saying, "Yes, you've got it," or, "That's just about what I meant, except that the real key is the fact that they didn't act as if they cared."

This paraphrasing technique allows the other person to affirm or correct your understanding of his communication. It also sends a message that indicates: "I'm trying to understand what you're saying." While restating or rephrasing is helpful at any time in the conversation, it is particularly appropriate after the employee has finished describing a major piece of the overall picture. It gives the supervisor a chance to summarize what he has heard thus far.

2. *Encouraging responses.* These are goads to or reinforcements of the employee's speaking. They are not designed to actually interrupt the flow. The conversational ball remains in the employee's court. He is communicating but needs a little encouragement

to go on. In this situation, the following types of remarks can be helpful: "Uh-huh," "Go on," "Tell me more," "I see," "What happened next?" "Really?" "I understand." These brief comments imply understanding. They do not indicate agreement but are said as a normal courtesy and let the other know that he is being encouraged to continue.

In our culture, a fundamental rule of communication is that we should only speak to another person for a limited period of time, usually not more than a couple of minutes, before we allow that person to say something in return. If we do not provide these encouraging, go-on comments, most employees will stop speaking. The temptation for the supervisor then is to start speaking, and at that moment the important objectives of counseling will have been lost: venting and diagnosis. By the use of these encouraging comments, the supervisor is sending a signal: "I'm understanding you; and while I'm inserting a brief comment just now, I do want you to continue with the flow of what you're trying to communicate to me." Keep the ball in their court.

3. *Silence.* It's been noted that since we have two ears and one mouth, that suggests a ratio! Silence is a powerful listening skill, in that it eloquently communicates that we want the other person to continue and that we are impressed with what he has said. When the employee comes to the end of his message, the supervisor could respond by simply remaining silent, perhaps nodding his head or maintaining a look of interest. These pregnant pauses are probably most appropriate when the employee has said something quite weighty or has expressed a strong emotion. At such times, silence can be a signal of respect: "I'm so impressed with what you've said that I don't know what to say"; or, "I have such respect for what you've just expressed that I don't want to intrude on that thought."

Silence creates a vacuum, and as the seconds quickly pass, it tends to force the person to begin speaking again. Because people follow Sherman's law, that "Whatever I say it is, there is always more," we know that they will often keep back the part of their story that is most sensitive. If the supervisor will maintain silence at the appropriate moment, with a look of openness and receptivity to what the employeee is saying, there is a good chance that the employee will start speaking. It may take as long as 15 seconds, but usually no longer, for the conversation to resume.

Summary

Every manager who has ever tried to help problem employees has noticed that such employees are unusually difficult to reach. Part of the problem stems from a perceptual deficiency that blocks these people from responding normally to the positive and negative feedback that are so effective in shaping the performance of nonproblem employees.

Although counseling is of limited value with such unresponsive employees, there are certain communication techniques the manager can employ to elicit valuable information that will enable him to better diagnose the nature and extent of the problem and make a more informed decision regarding a solution.

The manager must begin the communication process by establishing a firm connection with the troubled subordinate and becoming trusted by him (while keeping in mind that even these communication overtures may not succeed with a truly disturbed employee). The manager's communication stance throughout the process should be assertive — with the manager confronting candidly and openly, respectfully offering the employee an opportunity to upgrade performance. Both passivity (abdication of managerial responsibility with respect to problem employees) and aggressiveness (browbeating subordinates in hopes of forcing a behavior change) are to be avoided.

The manager must take into account three barriers to effective communication: those that are internal to the supervisor (such as lack of confidence, impulsiveness, and poor counseling skills), those found in the environment surrounding the communication (background distractions, failure to recognize that the message sent may not be the message received, and use of either emotionally provocative or incomprehensible language), and those internal to the employee (fear, anxiety, lack of candor, receptivity problems, and the like).

Through effective use of questioning and listening skills, the manager can do a great deal to overcome these barriers by structuring the communication so that the employee himself is able to cross these barriers and reach the manager. These skills serve two vital functions: (1) They enable problem employees to air their concerns, and (2) they enable a manager to better diagnose the situation.

The use of questioning skills can be thought of as "running the funnel" — guiding the conversation with the employee so it progresses from broad questions designed to give the manager the big picture to open-ended (*what, where, why, when, how* and *who*) questions, which channel the employee's responses more narrowly, yet without cutting off those responses (as could be the case with close-ended questions, which elicit a terse — and not fully informative — yes or no). From there, the communication focuses in even further on the problem situation through the use of specific questions that will clarify details and concludes with self-evaluation questions that invite the employee to paint in the emotional hues that color the situation for him. Passing through the funnel in this sequence will lay the groundwork between the manager and the employee that can enable the manager, in the latter stages of the conversation, to elicit details or emotionally charged information that would not have been forthcoming from the employee at the outset of the session.

The manager must complement these questioning techniques with listening skills to confirm that he is fully hearing the message that is being elicited from the employee. Chief among the listening skills — which can be thought of as a way to "grease the slide" of communication — are: restating/rephrasing, to enable the manager to check out his understanding; providing brief, encouraging responses that do not interrupt but merely prompt the employee to continue; and silence, to create a conversational vacuum that the other person will feel compelled to fill, quite possibly with crucial and more sensitive information that he may have been holding back.

9

Special Cases/Special Approaches

While this book provides a number of general models that should be considered in nearly all problem employee cases, there are some particular types of problems that call for specific approaches. We will briefly consider five groups here: the emotionally disturbed, absentees, alcoholics, substance abusers, and the accident-prone.

The Emotionally Disturbed

By the emotionally disturbed, I do not mean the person who is momentarily upset, but the person whose emotions are so disrupted as to make him unable to function fully. Such a person needs immediate attention, and the supervisor can be instrumental in keeping him from going over the edge.

Dr. Harry Levinson, of the Levinson Institute, is widely respected for his insights into applied psychology in the workplace.[1] His research has identified three major signs the supervisor can look for in determining whether an employee may be emotionally disturbed and in need of counseling:

1. *Look for personality extremes.* Most people under stress and experiencing emotional trouble do not flip-flop; they do not change their personality type. Rather, their normal character traits intensify. The shy person becomes reclusive and withdraws into a shell. The usually outgoing person becomes extremely extroverted and socializes with intensity. So look for the person who seems to be changing in the sense of amplifying or deepening who he is.

2. *Look for stress symptoms.* As a second stage, when the employee finds no relief by withdrawing into self or projecting outward through activity, he may start to show signs of anxiety, tension, facial redness, heavy perspiration, or become jittery or panicky. This second stage of disturbance can then lead to the third stage.

3. Look for the out-of-control person. If the employee is unable to cope with the anxiety, he may break down altogether and lose control of behavior and emotions. The employee's thinking may become irrational and will not make sense to other people. It is at this time that behavior patterns will change remarkably: the quiet person becoming noisy, the normally very orderly person becoming disorderly.

Emotional First Aid

When the manager or supervisor spots any of the above symptoms, Dr. Levinson suggests the administration of emotional first aid:

- *Step one:* Recognize the emotional disturbance. You don't have to be able to categorize it or label it, but if you're seeing a real change in or deterioration of behavior or personality, the symptoms of extreme anxiety, or anything that appears to be an emotional breakdown, then acknowledge that this is a person in trouble.
- *Step two:* Provide relief for the individual's acute distress by listening. The supervisor's major responsibility at this point is to give the employee a chance to vent some of the excess pressure. It is not a cure for the problem, but simply a way to get him calmed down for the moment.

In this counseling session, the manager has to make a basic decision about whether the problem seems solvable by the employee and the manager working jointly and utilizing the other resources the company may have available.

Key point: Cases that are beyond the limits of the manager's capability should be referred to a more specialized and appropriate source of help. The role of the manager at this point is not to try to solve the problem or play amateur psychologist, but to get this person to a professional who can provide meaningful assistance.

One way to judge whether the supervisor can help the emotionally disturbed employee directly, and to recognize the limitations of helping, is to use this rule of thumb: If you see no improvement after two listening sessions, the case should be reported to the company's employee assistance program administrator, the company physician, or other health workers, such as a company nurse. The referral approach the supervisor should take is that of having the troubled person talk to the professional as a source of additional help rather than suggesting in any way that the employee is not worth the supervisor's time or that his case is hopeless.

The Absentee

Professor P. J. Taylor, of London University, former medical director of Shell, found that 60 percent of absences were due to serious or chronic illness and another 20 percent to acute short-term illnesses, such as the flu.[2] (However, beware of the statistics cited, in that they are accurate only for the jobs measured in the particular corporations involved in the study.) The total of 80 percent of absences that Dr. Taylor found to be caused by chronic or short-term illnesses could be considered justifiable absences. That is, they represent a cost of doing business that is truly beyond the capability of the employee to control.

However, this is not true of the remaining 20 percent of absences, about half of which involve employees who are completely well but claim illness in order to get another day off, and the other half of which involve employees who feel slightly unwell and decide to stay home because of their bad attitude about the job. It is this 20 percent of the absenteeism that is subject to some management.

Generally speaking, absenteeism can be reduced by the following steps:

1. Define and enforce the rules governing absences in your organization.
2. Be as consistent as possible in applying penalties and sanctions, such as loss of pay for the time missed.
3. Keep accurate records of lost time and target any employee whose absences are exceeding the acceptable average. In some cases, this can be monitored by computer.
4. Determine with the employee why he is experiencing particular difficulties in getting to work on time or at all.

Usually, the supervisor tries to remedy the absenteeism problem through counseling. While some absentees will respond to counseling, others will not. Counseling has some probability of working for the following people:

1. Those whose pressures off the job are so strong that they affect the employees' commitment to get to work.
2. Employees whose work appears to them to be disagreeable and dissatisfying.
3. Employees whose working relationships with others are unpleasant and distasteful.
4. Those who develop a habit of absence or tardiness, not based on an underlying serious problem, and who could benefit from a straightforward "word to the wise."

On the other hand, it's been found that a counseling approach will probably not work with those employees for whom:

1. The pay level or the job itself holds no strong attraction.
2. Off-hours activities have a greater appeal than on-the-job activities.
3. The whole purpose of being absent is to inconvenience, punish, or disrupt the organization.

For this latter group of employees, discharge may be the only appropriate course of action.

The Alcoholic Employee

The best possibility of saving alcoholic employees is to recognize them in the early stages, try to gain their confidence, help them talk out their problems, and refer them to professionals in the field, starting first with the company's own health-care or employee assistance program, if one exists.

The most effective course is to approach suspected alcoholics with understanding and support, but be firm and confront the situation. Do not describe behavior in moral terms or accuse them of being alcoholic. The kinds of approaches necessary to rehabilitate alcoholics are beyond the scope of this work or of any manager's capability. Thus, the primary objective for the manager is to get the employee into the hands of treatment professionals.

Absenteeism and the Alcoholic

Contrary to long-standing belief, recent evidence suggests that alcoholics are not likely to be absent more often on Monday or Friday, nor are they tardy more often than nonalcoholics. Professor Harrison M. Trice, of Cornell University, who performed a major study of the job behavior of alcoholics, discovered that these widely held beliefs were not substantiated when an actual examination of alcoholic employees' attendance records was made. However, he suggests that the attendance record does remain a strong indicator of the presence of an alcoholic. Specifically, these points about attendance were found to apply to alcoholics:

1. Their overall absence rate will be higher than average. In fact, a high absence rate almost always accompanies an employee's development of drinking problems.
2. Their absences are spread out through the week, so as not to draw attention to the condition.
3. Partial absenteeism is frequent, with alcoholics often leaving prior to the end of the shift, even though they may have been at work on time at the beginning of the day.[3]

Approaching the Alcoholic

An excellent summary of the approach that should be taken by the supervisor is presented in a booklet entitled "The Supervisor's Guide on Alcohol Abuse," published by the U.S. Department of Health and Human Services. The following are some specific suggestions for how the supervisor should proceed:

1. The supervisor need not act apologetic about confronting the employee and bringing up the issue of alcoholism.
2. If a deterioriation in work performance, behavior, or attendance has been

noted, the employee should be asked for an explanation. He should be specifically questioned about the possibility of a drinking problem.

3. The supervisor should refrain from moralizing or implying that the employee has no right to drink (off the job, that is).

4. The supervisor should also refrain from asking the employee to drink less or make other changes in his or her consumption of alcohol.

5. Sometimes the employee will offer an excuse (or even several excuses) for the increased drinking (marital difficulties or sizable and pressing expenses, for instance). Since these are basically side issues, not directly job-related problems, the manager should not be distracted into attempting to help the employee cope with them. The manager must keep the focus on the primary concern: how the employee's drinking affects his job performance.

6. The problem employee may claim to be under a physician's care for alcoholism or to be attending counseling sessions; he may further claim that the problem is therefore under control. The employee may even go so far as to state that his consumption of alcohol was found by a health-care professional to be well within the limits of normal social drinking. Even granting the truth of these assertions, the supervisor shouldn't be deterred from actively pursuing the issue. Any health-care professional who became aware of the employee's deteriorated job performance would quite probably reconsider the seriousness of the problem and reassess whether the drinking was in fact under control.

7. The supervisor should not lose sight of the fact that the alcoholic employee is suffering from a disease and that, as with any other disease, the emphasis should be on treatment and rehabilitation, not on fault finding and moralizing.

8. At this point, suspension or discharge should be firmly raised by the supervisor as very real possibilities should the employee fail to control his work performance. The employee should also be told that he bears the responsibility for seeking professional help in managing the problem. The manager should approach the situation in a businesslike manner — making it clear that his actions are prompted strictly by a desire to help upgrade the employee's present unsatisfactory job performance.

9. The supervisor should make sure the company is doing everything it can to provide assistance to the problem drinker. The employee in question should definitely be referred to the employee assistance program or to health services, if these or similar functions exist with the organization. The supervisor should also ask the employee what help he needs and see whether it can be provided by the company or, if not, whether the company can refer the employee to an outside source of assistance.

As one EAP administrator who has had a 90 percent recovery rate among alcoholic government workers said:

> An employer — far better than wife, mother, minister, or social agency — can lead an alcoholic to treatment by *constructive coercion*. Give an employee every chance to take treatment, but make it clear that he must cooperate or lose his job. This has proved to be more effective than loss of friends or family.

"Constructive coercion" has been found to be the single most effective approach with these people because of the deep-seated nature of the problem they're battling.

Here's an example of how the counseling discussion might be handled:

Manager:	Ted, I think it's important for us to talk about your performance and where things stand. We've previously discussed your absence record, deadline problems, and the falloff in the quality of your work.
Employee:	So why bring it up again?
Manager:	I think what I'm seeing in your performance indicates a drinking problem, and I felt I should raise this possibility with you. Ted, I have a lot of respect for you, but you know things can't go on this way.
Employee:	What makes you think I've got a drinking problem? I mean, everybody drinks socially in this office, so why single me out?
Manager:	Well, there are several things that make me wonder. I *have* seen you drink pretty heavily at some of the functions we've attended together. Some others in the office have even commented on it, and with the other problems we've discussed, it makes for a plausible explanation.
Employee:	Well, you're wrong. I don't have a drinking problem.
Manager:	I'm not saying you do. I'm not an expert in these things, but I do owe it to you to tell you what I see and what the pieces of this puzzle look like to me. The company has a treatment program for this sort of problem, and I think you should talk to the program coordinator about your situation.
Employee:	I won't do it. You're saying I'm a drunk, and you can't make me enter that program.
Manager:	Ted, listen to me carefully. You do not have to enter the program, but if you don't get some help — and soon — to turn things around, you're not going to have a job here. The reason I'm talking to you about this is because I care about you. To the extent that drinking is part of the problem, this program could go a long way toward helping you salvage the situation.
Employee:	Are you saying that if I enter the program, I won't be fired?
Manager:	No, I'm saying that you have to get your attendance under control, meet deadlines, and bring your work up to normal performance standards. Participating in this program would indicate to me that you're making an effort to do that. Because I'm trying to support your effort to fix things, I'm suggesting this to you as a positive step. And I think you're man enough to face up to this thing. Will you do it?
Employee:	All right. But will you help me keep my job?
Manager:	Ted, that's exactly what I intend to aim for. You've got to understand that just completing the program isn't going to be enough; you've got to get the job shaped up, too. But entering the program buys you some

time and should make it easier for you to make the other things happen. Have we got a deal?

Employee: Yeah. Say, I appreciate your sticking with me on this. I guess it's time I started getting things together.

The Substance Abuser

While addiction among employees in the United States is a growing problem, there is some evidence suggesting that it is not as prevalent as one might suppose. Nonetheless, the drug experimentation of the 1970s has now become a multibillion-dollar epidemic. Because of the insidious and covert nature of the problem, many employers are left with nothing better than their own instincts to guide policy making. The best recommendation: *Assume you have a substantial minority of drug users on the payroll; then ask whether that makes a difference to your business.*

One thing is clear: A rapidly increasing number of employers think that they have an employee drug problem or that they have a need to protect their operations from new hires who might introduce drugs into their work settings. In 1982, approximately 10 percent of the *Fortune* 500 companies were screening for drugs in preemployment physicals or as part of a testing program for current employees. That number had grown to 30 percent by 1986. This trend toward trying to screen out drug users by means of urine tests or other drug tests before or during employment may offer some hope for the future — although substantial legal and ethical issues exist. These efforts seem appropriate for workers in particularly sensitive positions like those affecting national security; the health-care professions, where access is greater; and the like.

What to Look For

It is almost impossible for a drug user to maintain a regular attendance record. Therefore, many drug users tend to select temporary or irregular jobs, or lower-skill-level jobs that don't require their full capabilities. Other users — including those in management positions — seek excuses for nonperformance in their current jobs, blaming others or in other ways setting up conditions that will mask their failure.

Other behavioral symptoms of drug use tend to manifest themselves in terms of poor or erratic performance, forgetfulness, missing deadlines, not performing safely, or leaving work early. Also, the cost of the drug habit in many instances leads to theft.

As with the alcoholic, there may be physical symptoms of substance use: pale or flushed skin color, frequent trips to the bathroom or to some location other than the work site, clammy skin, dilated pupils, slow response time in conversation, general nervousness or agitation if the employee is using "uppers" or lethargy if using "downers."

Many of the same guidelines suggested for management of the alcoholic employee apply. The role of the supervisor is to establish contact, build a relationship and trust, and get the employee referred to competent professional help. Constructive coercion is called for because of the hold that the drug has over the person.

Most corporations have been more willing to work with alcoholics than with drug-addicted employees. This seems justified based on the illegality of most drugs. In other cases, employers see drug users as representing a greater threat or danger to the business. While alcoholism is now properly understood as a disease where employer support is appropriate, few employers have as much sympathy for drug users.

The Accident-Prone

All employees are at risk for accidents, but certain employees are accidents looking for someplace to happen. A psychological profile of accident victims has been developed, to help employers identify workers whose personality and life profile set them up to have accidents. In one firm, Aetna Casualty and Surety Company found that a person who filed a workers' compensation claim had a 40 percent probability of being involved in another accident on the job and again filing a claim.[4] When it comes to occupational injuries, repeaters are found in disproportionate numbers. It's important to understand that the accident-involved person is often an accident maker.

Dr. Gerald Jordan, of Du Pont, which has one of the best safety records of any company in the world, calls accident-proneness a form of mental illness:

> Our studies have revealed a small group of individuals around whom occupational injuries seem to cluster in disproportionate numbers. Obviously there is something more than hard luck plaguing a man whose career shows a long series of injuries. What's back of his trouble? The answer is that the accident maker is suffering from a form of mental illness so widespread that it may be found to some degree in most of us. . . . It is the failure of the employee as a whole person that is the core of his problem. He tends to evade the rules, both of working and of living. . . . In most cases the potential accident victim has a long service record and is well trained for his job. But all too often he's a victim of his own bottled-up emotions, which he turns against himself.[5]

The best course of action for accident-prone employees is to discover them early and refuse to pamper them. Anytime a supervisor sees a safety rule being violated, he should immediately jump into that situation. "Safety first" is a sound management philosophy in terms of preventing both injury and expense for the company. But beyond that, by continually enforcing that philosophy, the supervisor signals everyone in the workforce that he is not going to tolerate any employees who want to hurt themselves.

Said Du Pont's Dr. Jordan:

> In my opinion, the fact that a worker violates a safety rule is more important than why he violates it. Pampering the emotionally disturbed individual only serves to increase his demands, and at the same time aggravates the severity of his illness.[6]

Since the evidence is that the accident-prone employee is emotionally disturbed, counseling, referral to professionals, and if necessary, termination are the suggested courses of action.

Summary

Beyond the techniques applicable to problem employees in general, there are special approaches for dealing with particular types of problem employees.

Once the supervisor has spotted the typical signs of an emotionally disturbed worker, the supervisor's approach should be to acknowledge the disturbance and listen to the worker so he can blow off steam. It is important for the supervisor (1) to recognize when to call in outside assistance in dealing with an emotionally disturbed employee and (2) to be familiar with sources of professional help to which he can refer the troubled worker.

Of all workers who call in sick, one study found a malingering rate of approximately 20 percent, about half comprised of healthy workers and the other half comprised of slightly ill workers who didn't wish to bother coming in. This problem can by managed through strict enforcement of rules governing absenses and careful record keeping. Certain types of often-absent workers will respond to counseling, while other types won't. Members of this latter group may be candidates for termination.

Alcoholic workers can be identified through certain typical signs. When a drinking problem is suspected, the manager must firmly raise the issue with the employee and work with him to correct the problem — making it clear that continuation of the situation is unacceptable and that termination will result if the employee's performance is not brought up to standard.

From the supervisor's perspective, management of the substance abuser is similar to management of the alcoholic employee, although the covert nature of drug addiction makes it more difficult to get a handle on the presence and extent of the problem. The approach here is for the supervisor to be alert for the typical signs of substance abuse and refer the user to competent professional help.

It has been found that accident-prone employees fit a standard psychological profile and are in fact suffering from a form of mental illness. Such workers constitute a small group who are inclined to be accident repeaters, involved in a disproportionate number of job-related injuries. Very strict enforcement of safety rules, coupled with professional counseling, are the only effective approaches with such workers, with termination being reserved as an option for workers who fail to respond.

10

Formal Disciplinary Procedures

While disciplinary procedures are of value, they are required only when other more positive measures have failed. If the manager has used the correct management techniques designed to positively prevent problem behavior (thorough orientation and training, good supervision, effective communications, selective job assigning, and the like), and the person still fails to meet the standards, then the manager has no choice but to follow the steps of positive employee discipline. Sooner or later this means resorting to formal disciplinary procedures.

The major problem that one is confronted with in formal discipline is its apparent inconsistency with more positive supervisory values and behavior. Most supervisors would like to think of themselves as parental figures, coaches, teachers, counselors, friends. However, it is hard to maintain that image with employees when supervisors are also called upon to be judges and police officers. Nonetheless, experience with human beings at work shows that the more positive supervisory roles cannot be effectively carried out if supervisors don't also show that they can be firm about upholding behavior and performance standards. That is, people have to know that a manager will take disciplinary measures and enforce the rules with some form of sanctions designed to inflict punishment if the situation warrants it.

A basic rule of governance, whether in leading a nation or in managing an organization, is that those who are given leadership roles must maintain law and order. The bottom line is that people have to know that there is a bottom line! It is important for people not to think it is possible to "get away" with inappropriate behaviors. And that has been found to be a principle of behavior management in governing countries, raising teenagers, or running General Motors!

At work, it has been found that when rules are fair and are enforced, it strengthens the dynamics within the work group. When members of the work group believe that things should be done the right way, and believe that what is requested of them is appropriate, then they will tend to subscribe to these written and unwritten rules of conduct and also turn against employees who do not subscribe to them. That is, it helps to spell out what is unacceptable, because that provides a clearer definition of what is good. And to do good, ipso facto, is to be a winner in life and at work.

So while some managers shrink philosophically from the idea that discipline in the sense of sanctions and punishment can be good for discipleship, it has been found to be a practical necessity at work. It may very well be that the exception proves the rule — that the problem behavior that is nonresponsive to all other remedies and requires a more drastic approach shows the value of more positive management approaches and how responsive most people are to them.

Avoid Discipline When Possible

Yet I am not making a case for formal discipline with the idea in mind that we should occasionally hang some poor wretch from the organizational yardarm in order to set an example. I'm not advocating that we beat people into submission for their own good. In fact, the first principle of formal discipline is to avoid it whenever possible.

Out of the collective management experience, there have emerged a number of basic rules of the road for managing formal discipline:

1. *Avoid too many rules.* An excessive number of policies and regulations, particularly those that are unrelated to the job at hand, always cause more problems than they cure. A few sensible rules seem to have more value than lots of little rules that everybody ignores.
2. *Sell people on the rules.* People will work with you only when the rules that are adopted are reasonable and fair.
3. *Enforce the rules.* Law enforcement officials point out that laws are useless when they are unenforceable. If the rule can't be enforced, or if the rule isn't going to be enforced, do away with the rule.
4. *Don't substitute rules for management.* Never use formal disciplinary procedures if other, more obvious answers to the employee behavior problem are at hand. Don't punish people who need training or transfer or a different job assignment.
5. *Try communications one more time.* Many apparent disciplinary situations are often simply miscommunications or misunderstandings between the manager and the employee. Don't jump down people's throats if they simply haven't understood.

The Hot-Stove Rule

Douglas MacGregor, one of the first psychologists to discuss questions of motivation in a business environment, is credited with giving us the hot-stove rule. The rule suggests that the disciplinary process is analogous to touching a red-hot stove:

- *Immediacy.* When people burn their hand on a red-hot stove, they are sometimes angry not only with themselves but with the stove, as well. Nonetheless, they do learn the lesson about not touching the stove in the future because the burn is such a direct, immediate, and obvious consequence of the touching. There is no question about there being a cause-and-effect relationship here.
- *Warning.* The stove provided warning—since its surface was red, everyone could see that it was hot and could predict what would happen if they did touch it.
- *Consistency.* A stove is consistent in administering pain, because it burns every time that it's touched.
- *Impersonality.* The pain that results is impersonal. Anybody and everybody who touches the stove will get burned, regardless.

The key point of this analogy is understanding that the stove burns not because whoever touched it is bad but because he has violated the hard-and-fast laws of physics. In other words, the pain is directed against the act itself, not against the person. When the hot-stove rule is applied in a disciplinary setting, the employee may feel some resentment, but the counseling he's receiving is not a personal attack.

Are We Disciplining with Immediacy?

In thinking through how to apply these points in your organization, ask yourself these questions: Are we following the principle of immediacy of discipline? How quickly do we respond when we find that company rules or policy has been violated? Do we wait for the annual performance review and mention it then, carrying our knowledge of the infraction around internally with a sense of resentment in the meantime? Or do we call the offending employee in on the same day we see a problem and explain that the behavior is unacceptable? The employee may not like being confronted, but certainly confronting him right away is more likely to get results than postponing the inevitable. If we have to zap violators, let's do it immediately so they can learn from the experience and not confuse them by letting it slide until *mañana*.

Are We Disciplining with Advance Warning?

In the area of advance warning, have we done a good enough job of communicating what the rules and standards are? Have we published them? Have we covered them in training programs? Have they been referred to at appropriate times in unit meetings? Often what happens is that a policy is written and filed away in a dusty book, never to be seen again, and is only brought out, unfortunately, on certain occasions against certain individuals. This approach gets the company into legal trouble. If we're not going to enforce a policy, then we shouldn't have it.

We ought to think of policy and work rules the way we think of road signs. When driving, our behavior is guided by the unmistakable signs for stop, yield, merge, and so on. By following the signs, we protect all concerned, and in the event of an accident, our liability may be determined by what we were doing in relation to a road sign's instructions. In a sense, work rules and standards are nothing more than road signs governing behavior within the organization.

If some of the rules have not been enforced in your organization for some time, that doesn't mean that you can't begin enforcing them now. But I would strongly suggest that you not begin enforcement until after you have widely communicated that you're going to. In certain cases, courts and arbitrators have ruled that a precedent of nonenforcement had been established. What that means is that the rule had become invalid through disuse and was no longer applicable.

If you change rules, or if you intend to begin enforcing rules that haven't been in force, it would be appropriate to advise all employees of that, both in meetings and in writing. Give them sufficient understanding and time to adapt to the new or now-to-be-enforced rules.

Are We Disciplining with Consistency?

How consistent are we in applying discipline? One of the most common complaints expressed in opinion surveys is that supervisors apply the rules in an inconsistent or whimsical way. Charges of favoritism are leveled, and group morale suffers. Is the rule enforced every time? Or is it on-again, off-again enforcement? And are we enforcing the rule against everyone, regardless of title or status, and not exempting some people, including managers themselves, as if they were a privileged elite?

The question of consistency also concerns the severity of the punishment or discipline to be applied. Do some people get away with a warning while others are suspended for the same infraction? Was one employee fired for theft but another not? That the punishment should match the crime is an old standard of law, and it certainly applies in the disciplinary arena.

Consistency, of course, is hard to maintain and is particularly difficult when a number of different departments are involved. Some supervisors are more relaxed and others more stringent, and this leads to an unevenness in administration. Inconsistency in enforcement of the rules can be minimized, however, through supervisory-training programs and executive review.

While uniformly consistent application is desirable, it is not entirely possible. Perhaps one way of dealing with this is to ask, "Is this rule easy to enforce?" If the answer is yes, then enforce it against all violaters. If the answer is no, then an alternative would be to give awards to employees who live up not only to the letter but to the spirit of that rule. For example, it may be more effective to pay a bonus for perfect attendance than to dock people's pay for repeated absences. When thinking through sanctions, it should be remembered that sanctions can be either positive or negative, and consistency of application of a sanction doesn't necessarily mean that a punishment has to be applied. Perhaps a reward for those who are following the rules would be more appropriate.

Are We Disciplining Impersonally?

The fourth feature of the hot-stove rule was impersonality. By impersonality, we mean that the rule is applied against the behavior or the act, not against the person. We don't come on like Attila the Hun and say to the offender, "Aha! Late again, I see"; or, "I see that you're measuring up to your usual low standard performance." We are always courteous with people. Our stance is always one of respect for the individual but intolerance and nonacceptance of the problem behavior. So in a counseling discussion, we would focus on the issue of the person's being tardy and what caused that tardiness. "I notice that this latecoming has been a pattern just recently, and I'm wondering if you can explain to me why that is."

Impersonality represents, in a sense, a detached objectivity. Just as a physician would talk to a patient about symptoms he was manifesting and what could be done to alleviate the condition, that is the proper approach for the supervisor, as well. The doctor does not say, "You're bad because you have this disease"; or, "I don't like you because you have this disease." To approach problem employees on a personal level and impugn their motives or call into question their ethics is not going to change their behavior. Instead, it will provoke a combative response, generate a very powerful emotional resistance, and almost guarantee future noncompliance with the rules. While such employees may make us feel angry, in that they have let us and the team down, to approach them in a personally demeaning way is certain to be ineffective.

Keep in mind the objective: We are trying to change behavior. In following the hot-stove approach, our use of formal discipline should burn people immediately, it should burn them every time they exhibit problem behavior, it should burn regardless of who they are, and it should burn without our becoming emotionally involved.

Progressive Discipline

The concept of progressive discipline is used when an organization applies penalties for either substandard performance or violations of work rules. These penalties become increasingly severe as the infraction is repeated or gets worse. A typical progressive-discipline approach would include three to five levels of severity.

In a five-level system, the process usually begins with a verbal warning. Nothing is put in writing, but the employee is told what the problem is with his behavior and that it should not be repeated. The second level is a written reprimand—a note either sent to the employee or placed in the employee's file with his knowledge. The third level is a second written reprimand. The fourth level is suspension, usually for a one- to three-day period. The final level is discharge.

A three-step progressive-discipline process would usually shorten the chain of events by giving the employee a verbal warning, then a written reprimand, and finally, suspension or discharge. In most organizations, progressive discipline is spelled out as a management policy. In other settings, it is written into a union contract. If you want to institute a progressive system, I'd recommend that you have no more than three levels and that you make provision for skipping these based on the severity of the offense or collective management judgment. In other words, keep it short and somewhat flexible.

What About the Union?

The presence of a union usually brings both positive and negative forces to bear in the discipline arena. On the positive side, it ensures clear-cut disciplinary procedures throughout the organization. The steps that management can take to deal with poor performance are clearly enunciated and communicated to all union members. On the negative side, a union can aggravate the situation by insisting on time delays, appeals, and third-party representation and by injecting a much more legalistic tone into the proceedings.

A union's involvement usually includes a one- to three-level appeal process as part of overall grievance handling. Also, the union presence severely compromises the manager's role as enforcer and judge. The presence of a union can turn the discipline arena into a nightmare, with grievances being filed, formal suspensions in effect, and so forth. The paperwork and time consumption involved in dealing with these matters are horrendous. Nonetheless, while a union's disciplinary procedures drastically restrict what a supervisor can do, the workings of this system can eventually remove from the organization those who deserve dismissal.

One of the reasons discipline in a union environment often goes sour is that the other elements of positive discipline are missing. Discipline applied in an atmosphere of antagonism doesn't work. It is instructive to note that a number of nonunion organizations that practice positive discipline have borrowed the ideas of progressive discipline, appeal steps, and even employee representation through ombudspersons, from practices that were largely originated by the labor movement.

Disciplinary Action Can Be Overturned

An examination of court and arbitration rulings shows that supervisors' disciplinary actions have been overturned when any of the following conditions exist:

1. *Insufficient evidence.* When the manager's accusations or beliefs about what the employee is supposed to have done are not founded in fact, when there are no witnesses, no production records, no lost-time records, then the manager may find his disciplinary decision being overruled.

2. *Inadequate warning.* When there is no policy or there is a policy that is not publicized, or when the employee received no warning that he was in violation of the rule prior to a penalty's being imposed, then the courts have ruled that warnings were nonexistent or inadequate.

3. *Too-severe punishment.* Organizations or managers who do not use a progressive-discipline approach and instead go directly to suspension or termination without due process have sometimes found that their actions are looked on unfavorably by the courts. This is especially true when the disciplinary action in question involves a first offense or a worker who has an otherwise good work record, or when the punishment simply does not seem to fit the crime.

4. *Actions based on prejudice.* Any act of discrimination will place the supervisor's recommendation for discipline in jeopardy. These days many employees are aware of this and will cry discrimination when none exists in order to distract attention from the real issue. Prejudice and bias need not only include covered categories such as race, age, or sex but can also involve accusations of an unwarranted preference for certain educational or experience levels, physical appearance, and so on.

5. *No clear-cut violation of policy.* An employee may act contrary to the intent or spirit of prohibitions against similar or related behaviors that are covered in the policy, but if that policy does not specifically prohibit the action for which the employee is being punished, it may later prove difficult to persuade the courts to uphold a disciplinary action that was, strictly speaking, not justifiable.

6. *Inadequate documentation.* A supervisor who claims to have followed a progressive-discipline approach but can produce no documentation will find that his story is considered suspect. As stated throughout this book, keeping written records is extremely important, and their very absence can undermine a case that the supervisor is trying to establish.

Formal discipline is only a part of the overall process of positive discipline. Used by itself, it creates a legalistic and confrontational atmosphere. But used in conjunction with, and sometimes parallel to, other efforts that are supportive and developmental, formal discipline can make a very powerful contribution toward channeling behavior.

Examples of Company Procedures

The following figures reflect different approaches to a formal discipline process. They are good examples of how organizations can adapt the principles of progressive discipline to their specific needs. The exhibits come from three organizations and are reproduced with permission. Company names have been deleted to preserve confidentiality.

Figures 4 and 5. These two forms, which start on pages 124 and 125, show two different but related approaches taken with violators, based on whether their act was *behavioral* or against established *work rules.* What is particularly useful in this scheme is that it shows exactly what types of infractions will result in corrective action. It also demonstrates a willingness to work with people on their behavioral failings but provides a very short leash when it comes to violations of work rules.

Figure 6. This material, which starts on page 126, is extracted from an employee handbook. It is clear that this organization has done a good job of taking care that

(Text continues on p. 141.)

Figure 4. Corrective action form: behavior standard violations.

Employee's
Name ———————————— Department ——————————— Date ——————

Violations of behavior standards are corrected through a progressive disciplinary procedure.

( )   1. Excessive absenteeism.
( )   2. Excessive tardiness.
( )   3. Job duties performed below standard.
( )   4. Abusive physical behavior.
( )   5. Sleeping on the job.
( )   6. Disregarding personal hygiene or standards of dress and appearance.
( )   7. Unauthorized personal visits or telephone calls.
( )   8. Discourteous or inappropriate interpersonal relations.
( )   9. Parking in unauthorized parking zone/failure to display parking sticker.
( ) 10. Failure to follow safety practices.
( ) 11. Other behavior problems.

DISCIPLINARY STEP	First Discussion ( )	Second Discussion ( )	Probation ( )	Suspension ( )	Discharge ( )
DATE	__/__/__	__/__/__	__/__/__	__/__/__	__/__/__
TIME	————	————	————	————	————
ACTION TO BE TAKEN					
EMPLOYEE'S COMMENTS					

The employee's signature indicates that this matter was discussed with him/her and does not necessarily mean that the employee agrees with what is stated.

Employee's Signature ————————————————————— Date ——————

Supervisor's Signature ————————————————————— Date ——————

For probation, suspension, and discharge actions:
Reviewed by:
Personnel Director ————————————————————— Date ——————

Department Director ————————————————————— Date ——————

Vice-President ————————————————————— Date ——————

Figure 5. Corrective action form: work rule violations.

Employee's
Name _____ Department _____ Date _____

Violations of work rules are regarded as major infractions subject to immediate termination of employment.

( ) 1. Mistreatment of patient.
( ) 2. Theft, reasonable basis for suspicion of theft, or attempted theft.
( ) 3. Willful destruction of property.
( ) 4. Assault with intent to do bodily injury.
( ) 5. Insubordination: refusal to perform assigned work.
( ) 6. Willful breach of confidentiality.
( ) 7. Sexual harassment.
( ) 8. Use of alcohol or drugs on hospital premises or reporting to work under their influence to the extent that job performance is in any way impaired or to the extent that others are aware of their use.
( ) 9. Willful falsification of personnel, time and attendance, or other hospital records.
( ) 10. Solicitation or distribution.
( ) 11. Possession of firearms or other dangerous weapons on hospital premises.
( ) 12. Violation of major safety rules.
( ) 13. Any absence without notification to supervisor prior to shift start.

DISCIPLINARY   Suspension   Discharge
ACTION   ( )   ( )

Date _____ Time _____

INVESTIGATION _____
RESULTS _____

_____

EMPLOYEE'S _____
COMMENTS

_____

The employee's signature indicates that this matter was discussed with him/her and does not necessarily mean that the employee agrees with what is stated.

Employee's Signature _____ Date _____

Supervisor's Signature _____ Date _____

Reviewed by Personnel Director _____ Date _____

Department Director's Signature _____ Date _____

Vice-President's Signature _____ Date _____

For additional space, use the reverse of this form.

Figure 6. Selected passages from an employee handbook.

EMPLOYEE DISCIPLINE

I. *Policy.* Corrective discipline is the responsibility of the supervisor and is intended to help the employee develop a more acceptable form of behavior.

   A. Disciplinary action should be carefully considered to determine whether infractions are in part the result of:

      1. Poor supervision
      2. Improper placement
      3. Inadequate training
      4. Compelling personal problems

   B. Most forms of problem behavior can be dealt with successfully without resorting to penalty-type measures. Employee counseling, additional training, or temporary change in work assignment may resolve the difficulty.

   C. Where it is necessary to use corrective measures:

      1. Methods chosen must fit the individual situation.
      2. Action taken must be timely, reasonable, and understood by the employee.
      3. Written notices given employees must be specific as to the reasons for the action and a time frame for improvement identified.
      4. Supervision must be firm and consistent in the actions taken.

II. *Types of disciplinary actions.* There are three possible steps the supervisor may take in maintaining discipline after counseling has failed:

   A. First, a verbal warning as part of a normal relationship between supervisor and worker. This is appropriate for minor infractions after counseling has failed. The problem must be pointed out to the employee; he/she should understand the necessity for correcting his/her behavior; a full discussion by both the supervisor and the worker is desirable. Any correction should not be made in the presence of other employees. A written statement should be placed in the employee's chronological record indicating that a verbal warning has been given.

   B. Second, a written letter of reprimand or probation. This action is appropriate for a more serious infraction or repeated infractions. The employee is given both a verbal and written reprimand to ensure that he/she understands what the infraction was and to provide a written record of the matter. A copy will be made a part of the employee's personnel record. A letter of reprimand should include:

      1. A complete and specific description of the offense.
      2. A restatement of past offenses, with corrective action taken.
      3. A statement that repetition of the offense will result in more severe disciplinary action.
      4. A statement of the time given the employee to correct deficiencies. (In the case of probation, the period normally will be 90 days.)

Figure 6. (Continued)

C. Third step, discharge of the employee, is the action taken after continued failure to attain the desired change in the worker's conduct or behavior; this action may be taken initially for more serious misconduct or infraction of rules. Department directors and administrative staff shall furnish proper documentation of the events to the Director or Assistant Director of Employee Relations for joint consideration and decision. A termination check must be given to the employee when he is discharged.

Discharge may also result when performance is below standard. Poor quality of work, inadequate quantity, and taking too long to perform the work may all be sufficient justification for discharge. The employee retains the right to reply and to use the hospital grievance procedure if he feels the discharge penalty is too severe.

During new-employee or disciplinary probation periods, work infractions or misconduct may be cause for immediate discharge.

D. Suspension: In place of, in addition to, or as a prestep to any step of the disciplinary procedure, suspension without pay (up to five working days) may be invoked by the supervisor as a stopgap measure — it fills the gap between too hasty action and none at all. Suspension is used only until the hospital can consider the case against the employee and he has had an opportunity to reply to the accusations. If the case against the employee is dropped, the employee is entitled to immediate reinstatement with back pay for hours suspended. If the case is substantiated, the suspension will stand, and such other disciplinary action as outlined in this policy, including discharge, may be invoked.

III. *Additional table of penalties.* The proper functioning of any institution requires the publication and use of a uniform set of rules for employees. The majority of our employees normally abide by established rules. A few will not observe regulations or rules unless they are forewarned of specific penalties. The following table of penalties may be used for successive rule infractions. In any given case, the circumstances may dictate a greater or lesser penalty rather than the order suggested here, and nothing in this policy will be construed to prevent a lesser or greater penalty's being imposed for any infraction of regulations, rules, or standards of conduct.

USUAL DISCIPLINARY ACTION

Key: VW = Verbal warning
WR = Written reprimand or probation
D = Discharge

OFFENSE	DISCIPLINARY ACTION		
	FIRST	SECOND	THIRD
1. Repeated tardiness, absenteeism, and abuse of lost-time privileges	VW or WR	WR or D	D

Figure 6. *(Continued)*

	DISCIPLINARY ACTION		
	FIRST	**SECOND**	**THIRD**
2. Discourteous treatment of patients, visitors, or other personnel	VW, WR, or D	WR or D	D
3. Insubordination (refusal to follow instructions or accept job assignments from a supervisor or properly designated hospital authority)	VW, WR, or D	WR or D	D
4. Late call (failure to call in on time when unable to report for duty as scheduled)	VW	WR	D
5. Incompetent performance of duties or neglect of duty	VW, WR, or D	WR or D	D
6. Evidence of possession of liquor or drug-substance abuse	WR or D	D	
7. Theft, regardless of value	WR or D	D	
8. Conduct endangering the life, safety, or health of others			
• Deliberate or willful	WR or D	D	
• Careless or negligent	VW, WR, or D	WR or D	D
9. Possession of unauthorized weapons on hospital premises	WR or D	D	
10. Failure to respect the confidential nature of hospital records and information about patients	WR or D	D	
11. Altering, removing, damaging, destroying, or improperly using hospital property			
• Negligent	VW, WR, or D	WR or D	D
• Deliberate	WR or D	D	
12. Malicious gossip about any employee, patient, physician, or hospital representative	VW	WR	D

Figure 6. (Continued)

| | DISCIPLINARY ACTION | | |
	FIRST	SECOND	THIRD
13. Dishonesty, including falsification or omission of any information pertaining to personal or business records, employment applications, and information on physical and mental condition	WR or D	D	
14. Accepting monetary tips	VW or WR	D	
15. Violation of parking policies (after three citations)	WR	Final WR	D
16. Solicitation: Employees are not permitted to solicit for donations or to sell any item to others (authorized functions would not apply)	VW or WR	WR or D	D
17. False recording of hours worked; falsification of or tampering with time cards	WR or D	D	
18. Leaving the premises or unauthorized absence from the work unit during a scheduled working day without permission of supervisor	WR	D	
19. Immoral or unprofessional conduct	WR or D	D	
20. Inability to work with others	VW	WR	D
21. Persistently uncooperative behavior	VW	WR	D
22. Failure to maintain a professional appearance	VW	WR	D
23. Sleeping on duty	WR	D	
24. Gambling on duty	WR	D	
25. Personal phone calls	VW	WR	D
26. Refusal to work overtime in an emergency situation without sufficient cause	VW or WR	WR or D	D
27. Sexual harassment	WR or D	D	

The above list of offenses is not intended to be all-inclusive.

Figure 6. *(Continued)*

RESIGNATION

At least two weeks' notice is required of all employees who resign; four weeks' notice is required for all department heads and supervisors. This advance notice must be written, dated, and addressed to your department head stating the reasons for leaving. Failure to give this written notice disqualifies you from being considered for reemployment. Exceptions to disqualification must be approved by a Vice-President and the Director of Employee Relations.

An employee who resigns after completion of probation is eligible for payment of all unused sick-leave time at his/her regular salary. Health insurance, dental insurance, disability insurance, and life insurance are discontinued. However, the employee may elect to convert the health insurance and life insurance to an individual policy. Information is available in the Personnel Department regarding conversion. Some pension benefits may be available to employees who resign after at least five years of continuous service. Credit union membership and participation may continue indefinitely at your own choosing, and a tax-sheltered annuity plan may be transferred if you go to work for another tax-exempt organization that has a tax-sheltered annuity program.

Any employee absent for three consecutive scheduled working days without notification will be considered to have voluntarily terminated employment.

SEPARATION

Sometimes an employee may be asked to leave for reasons other than disciplinary action. These are usually separations of mutual consent between the hospital and the employee and may involve such factors as inability to perform work duties, inability to get along with co-workers, poor health, etc.

An employee may be given the option of resigning rather than being discharged in this instance. A two-week (or four-week, depending upon job classification) notification period may or may not be allowed. An employee separated under these circumstances may be considered eligible for reemployment in another area of the hospital.

Employees who have passed new-employee probation and have been separated are eligible for payment of unused sick-leave time, which will be included in the last pay check.

SUSPENSION

Should disciplinary action be needed for infraction of work rules, an employee may be suspended for up to five working days without pay instead of being immediately discharged. This is true during investigation of a suspected infraction, as well. If after review by the department head, Director of Employee Relations, and appropriate Vice-President, the suspension is upheld, salary will not be paid for this period. The decision to either reinstate or discharge the employee after the five-day maximum suspension will be made in view of all evidence, the employee's behavior and efforts to improve, and the seriousness of the offense. If discharge is the end result, no wages will be paid for the period of suspension.

A grievance committee hearing may be requested by a suspended employee. If the committee should rule in favor of the employee, he/she will be reinstated immediately, back wages will be paid, and sick-leave accrual will be credited for that period of suspension.

Figure 6. (Continued)

An employee may also be suspended for an indefinite period of time pending investigation of and/or trial for an alleged criminal offense. If such a suspension is instituted and the court rules in favor of the accused employee, he/she may be reinstated.

DISCHARGE

If an employee is discharged, only those wages earned up to the time of discharge will be paid. However, the hospital reserves the right to withhold from an employee's terminal pay check an amount equal to or representative of the cost of replacing all hospital property or uniforms issued but damaged or not returned, or an amount equal to any outstanding balance for services rendered.

If a discharge has been recommended for disciplinary reasons during probation, the hospital will withhold payment of sick hours as a terminal benefit. In such case the two- (or four-) week notification period will also be waived.

EXIT INTERVIEW

Every person leaving employment for any reason must complete a termination questionnaire and have an exit interview with the department head. The Personnel Department may conduct an exit interview if requested by either the departing employee or the institution.

Administration is interested in knowing what employees think of the organization as a place in which to work. Facts gained from exit interviews are helpful in evaluating existing conditions and can result in improvement of working conditions, point out personnel problems, and possibly reduce turnover. The employee's signature is required on the exit interview form.

Figure 7. Disciplinary policy statements and supporting materials.

TERMINATIONS

Statement of Intent

To give fair and considerate treatment to all terminating employees.

Responsibilities

Manager:

1. Arranges for termination of employees.

2. Recommends discharge action when needed.

3. Conducts a final exit interview with the terminating employee. (Completes termination checklist in termination packet.)

Personnel Administrator:

Advises manager on termination procedures, legal implications, etc.

Practices

1. During the employee's termination interview, his/her position with respect to benefit plans, reemployment status, or any other pertinent information is reviewed.

2. There are five types of terminations:

   a. *Voluntary quits.* These are such causes as ill health, moving out of town, pregnancy, dissatisfaction with job or pay, or desire to enter another business.
   b. *Reduction in workforce.* If a reduction in the workforce should ever become necessary, consideration will be given to length of service, performance, and job requirements.
   c. *Discharge.*
   d. *Death.* The manager should notify the Personnel Administrator to assist in initiating the proper handling of group life insurance and other plans.
   e. *Retirement.*

3. The termination date is normally recorded as the *last day actually worked.* It is not extended by vacation allowance or other factors.

4. Employees who voluntarily quit only receive compensation for unused vacation and back pay.

Figure 7. (Continued)

5. In all cases of pregnancy, the employee may elect to resign or, with the approval of the manager, request a leave of absence.

6. See policy with regard to dismissal compensation.

7. Letters and verbal inquiries for information concerning terminated employees should be referred to the manager or Personnel Administrator. "To Whom It May Concern" letters are of little value and should be discouraged.

DISCHARGE

Statement of Intent

To discharge an employee whose performance or behavior is not in keeping with company standards, but only after a review of all the facts reveals that all reasonable corrective efforts have failed. In cases of gross misconduct, however, immediate discharge may be ordered.

Responsibilities

Manager:

1. Recognizes below-standard performance and potential failures among employees, especially during the early period of employment.

2. Sees that all reasonable corrective efforts are made and that proper warnings have been issued.

3. Recommends to General Manager an office employee's discharge if all appropriate corrective efforts fail.

4. Contacts the Personnel Administrator to inform him of intent to terminate an office employee.

5. Personally informs the employee of his discharge if it is approved and explains the reasons for the action in a proper spirit. This responsibility *cannot* be delegated to any staff member.

6. Conducts an exit interview with the discharged employee, explaining the application of benefit plans, final pay check, references, etc. (See checklist in termination packet.)

7. Discusses any aspect of the case that the employee wishes in order to assure his understanding.

Figure 7. (Continued)

General Manager:

    Approves all decisions regarding the discharge of an employee.

Personnel Administrator:

    The Personnel Administrator should be consulted prior to informing the employee to assure proper documentation and adherence to policy and practices.

Practices

1. When an employee's performance or conduct is contrary to the best interests of the company, and he is unwilling or unable to improve within a reasonable period of time after notice or warning, discharge should be considered as the wisest course of action.

2. As most performance problems do not occur overnight, it is expected that an employee will receive at least two warnings from the manager, accompanied by counseling intended to help correct the problem. The first warning and final warning should be in writing, outlining the problem(s), summarizing previous discussions of the problem(s), outlining and establishing objectives and timetables to be met.

3. At the time the written final warning is issued to an employee, the Personnel Administrator should be contacted to inform him of the situation.

4. Generally, a manager, General Manager, or the Personnel Administrator will support a recommendation to discharge an office employee if the following is revealed:

    a. The employee received at least two written warnings concerning his performance.
    b. The employee was told exactly what performance or behavior was expected, what was being done wrong, what to do to improve, and what would happen if no improvement resulted. *All of this should be documented in writing.*
    c. The employee was not held to or expected to meet unreasonable standards of performance or conduct.
    d. The employee had reasonable opportunity and amount of assistance to improve.
    e. Discharge is the appropriate course of action for the failure to make the required improvement.

5. If the recommendation for discharge is approved, all of the terms of the separation should be agreed upon in advance by the General Manager and the Personnel Administrator. The circumstances of each individual case should be considered in determining the timing, dismissal compensation, and assistance to be given in helping the employee find other employment.

6. There are certain acts of dishonesty, negligence, insubordination, and other acts of commission or omission that are such grave deviations from company standards of performance and conduct that summary dismissal is justified. It may be enough to establish the employee's guilt of the offense and that the offense warrants immediate dismissal. This action must be endorsed by both the General Manager and the Personnel Administrator.

Figure 7. *(Continued)*

EXAMPLE ONLY

To: Subject: Performance Problem Warning
From: Date:

To review the discussion of your performance problems held on _____ , it was stated that if you did not develop and maintain an acceptable performance record, you would be placed on a written First Warning status. Since this talk, the following performance problems have continued to exist:

1. You have been absent three (3) times within the last month without contacting the office and/or your manager explaining the absence.

2. You have left the office early on five (5) occasions and once when you were alone in the office put the phones on the answering service prior to normal closing hours at 4:30 p.m.

3. Your interpersonal relationships with the other two members of the office staff are continuing to cause a great deal of tension within the office, which directly affects the ability of the office to function in providing services to our customers.

Since you have failed to correct the performance problems that we discussed on _____ , I am placing you on written First Warning status. This probationary status will be in effect for three (3) months.

The guidelines for this warning period are as follows:

1. First Warning will be in effect from _____ to _____ .

2. During this warning period, you will have no unexcused absences. If you must be absent, you must inform me of your absence.

3. You are required to keep the office open from 8 a.m. to 4:30 p.m., Monday through Friday, and never to put the office on answering service prior to normal closing.

4. You will be required to work on your interpersonal relationships with other members of the office staff to reduce tension.

In the event you fail to comply with the First Warning guidelines at any time during the First Warning period, you may be placed on written Final Warning status. Should you encounter difficulties in complying with these guidelines, or if unusual circumstances occur, please discuss them with me.

Figure 7. (Continued)

At the end of the First Warning period on _____, your attendance and special written performance will be reviewed by me and discussed with you. Recommendations as to your future status will be made at that time.

_____   _____
Employee's Signature   Date

_____   _____
Manager's Signature   Date

_____   _____
General Manager's Signature   Date

Comments by Employee and/or Management:

Figure 7. *(Continued)*

EXAMPLE ONLY

To: Subject: Final Performance Warning
From: Date:

You have failed to comply with the guidelines outlined in the first performance problem warning issued on ———— .

Because you have continued to violate the written guidelines, you are being placed on Final Warning status effective ———— .

This probationary status will be in effect for three (3) months. The guidelines for the Final Warning period are as follows:

1. During this warning period, you will have no unexcused absences. If you must be absent, you must inform me of your absence.

2. You are required to keep the office open from 8:00 a.m. to 4:30 p.m., Monday through Friday, and never to put the office on answering service prior to normal closing.

3. You will be required to work on your interpersonal relationships with other members of the office staff to reduce tension.

In the event you fail to comply with the Final Warning guidelines, you may be subject to discharge. Should you encounter difficulties in complying with these guidelines, or if unusual circumstances occur, please discuss them with me.

Your performance record will be evaluated by management and discussed with you at the end of the Final Warning period on ———— . Your progress in following these guidelines will be reviewed and/or recommendations for your future status will be made at that time.

_____   _____   _____
Employee's Signature   Date   General Manager's Signature

_____   _____
Manager's Signature   Date

Comments by Employee and/or Management:

Figure 7. *(Continued)*

MANAGER'S CHECKLIST FOR EFFECTIVE DISCIPLINARY COUNSELING

PLEASE COMPLETE <u>BEFORE</u> TAKING ACTION

EMPLOYEE'S NAME: _____ SERVICE DATE: _____

INCIDENT: (An accurate statement of what happened and others involved.)
Be specific — no opinions.

_____

_____

_____

_____

WHAT DO YOU WANT TO CORRECT?

_____

_____

_____

_____

BACKGROUND INFORMATION:

_____ Has the employee had a chance to tell his/her side of story?

_____ Did you talk to the employee in private?

_____ Was the employee aware of the policy, procedure, or practice?

_____ Was the policy, procedure, or practice published in writing?

_____ Was it properly posted and communicated?

_____ Was the policy, procedure, or practice in effect?

_____ How long was the policy, procedure, or practice in effect?

_____ How consistently is the policy, procedure, or practice enforced?

Figure 7. (Continued)

_____ What has been done in similar cases?

_____ Is this employee being singled out?

_____ Any evidence of this violation's being overlooked?

_____ Did the employee have any previous warning?

_____ What previous corrective action was taken with this employee before the incident?

PROPOSED ACTION:

_____ Informal Warning.

_____ First Warning notice.

_____ Final Warning notice.

_____ Demotion.

_____ Discharge.

_____ Does punishment fit offense?

_____ Will measure prevent recurrence?

_____ Will measure encourage better performance?

_____ What effects will measure have on the individual?

_____ What effect will measure have on other members of the work group?

_____ What problems could result if this type of violation continued?

_____

_____

_____

_____

_____   _____

Manager's Signature   Date

Figure 7. (Continued)

DISMISSAL COMPENSATION

Statement of Intent

To assist with the financial adjustment of regular employees who are terminated as a result of action initiated by the company, except in cases of discharge or gross misconduct.

Responsibilities

Manager:

1. Determines an employee's eligibility for dismissal compensation and recommends the amount.

2. Discusses such cases with the General Manager.

3. After a decision has been made, discusses the amount of dismissal compensation with the employee during the final exit interview and informs the employee that this compensation will be in his final pay check.

Personnel Administrator:

Maintains consistent application of this policy throughout the organization.

Practices

1. *Eligibility for Dismissal Compensation*

    a. *Dismissal compensation is paid only when the separation is initiated by the company.*
    b. Dismissal compensation is normally paid only to regular employees with more than three months of service.
    c. Employees discharged for gross misconduct — such as theft, deliberate action to provoke discharge, or insubordination — do not usually receive dismissal compensation.
    d. Terminations at the end of a leave of absence are regarded as voluntary quits, and no dismissal compensation is paid.

2. *Amount of Dismissal Compensation*

    a. The following are the minimum amounts of dismissal compensation for regular full-time employees:

        ☐ Less than three months of service: none.

        ☐ Three to twelve months of service: 1 weeks' base pay.

        ☐ Twelve months or more: 2 weeks' base pay.

Figure 7. *(Continued)*

    b. Part-time employees will receive a percentage of dismissal compensation based on their actual hours worked.

    c. Dismissal compensation in excess of the minimum amounts is determined on an individual basis and should be based on the following factors:

        (1) Reason for dismissal

        (2) Family responsibilities

        (3) Overall performance

        (4) Length of service with the company

        (5) Age

---

employee communications happen! By clearly laying out the logic and philosophy of the organization along with the procedural steps that will be followed, it also represents something more than just a listing of problem behaviors.

Figure 7. In this example, which starts on page 132, the organization wanted to ensure that problem employees were handled quickly due to the small number of employees working in any single location. Here the emphasis is on the wording of written warnings in order to clearly communicate to problem employees what has to be improved.

In this decentralized operation, the checklist was particularly useful for the manager's review, since the personnel department was not immediately available.

Summary

While formal disciplinary procedures must be regarded as a last resort and are to be avoided whenever possible, they do have their place as a means of enforcing standards of behavior and performance with certain recalcitrant employees. Formal disciplinary procedures serve to tell such workers where the bottom line is.

Douglas MacGregor's hot-stove rule provides effective guidelines for the disciplinary process. In brief, the rule holds that discipline must immediately follow the infraction (just as the red-hot stove's burn immediately follows a careless touch), the discipline must be preceded by advance warning (just as the hot stove's glow indicates danger), the discipline must be consistently administered (just as the hot stove burns all who touch it, every time they touch it), and the discipline must be meted out impersonally (just as the stove burns without becoming emotionally involved with its victims).

As a means of putting the hot-stove rule into practice, many companies have progressive-discipline systems, commonly five-level and three-level systems. Of these, the three-level system is recommended for its simplicity and brevity. Whatever the number of levels chosen, the system should be designed for flexibility.

While the presence of a union ensures that uniform disciplinary procedures exist and are widely communicated throughout the organization, the union can often considerably complicate the functioning of a formal disciplinary apparatus — burdening the process with bureaucracy and legalistic overtones and greatly hampering the supervisor's freedom of action. However, even with a union's involvement, it is eventually possible to appropriately remove problem employees from the system.

In administering formal disciplinary sanctions, managers should keep in mind that such action can be overturned on a number of grounds (inadequate warning, insufficient evidence, excessive severity, prejudice, and so on). In taking action under a formal disciplinary system, managers must be certain to "cover all the bases" so that their action will be upheld, in the event that its legitimacy is ever challenged.

11

Power Counseling: The Last Talk

While the technique we are about to consider is sometimes called power counseling, what it really is is the shape-up-or-ship-out discussion that is the last conversation you have with an employee about improving his behavior or performance. This technique differs markedly from normal performance counseling, which is more conversational and relaxed. This is not the usual conversation where you simply say, "I'd like to call this deficiency or problem to your attention, and I want you to take care of it." This is not the simple little warning, "I want you to knock this off." This is the *last* real effort that you're going to make to reach this person.

Having such a conversation is not always appropriate. In a case where you've gotten so disgusted with the person that you want to terminate him or her, then I would suggest that you proceed with termination and not hold this last-ditch counseling session. This conversation is appropriate only if you buy the premises on which it's based. If you accept the assumptions that underlie this performance-counseling system, then you may have some good success with it. If you don't accept the premises, then simply going through the motions of the technique will be to no avail.

This is a very powerful counseling approach. Variations of this approach have been used with alcoholics when nothing else has been able to get through to them, with delinquent teenagers when parents are at the end of their rope — a technique known as "tough love." Let me acknowledge here the outstanding contribution of Dr. Mark Silber, who developed this technique for work settings. Much of what I'll be reporting here is based on Dr. Silber's experience as a practicing organizational and industrial psychologist.

As its name implies, the power-counseling technique indeed has great power. It is, in layperson's terms, what might be referred to as psychosurgery. It's an advanced technique. And because of its power, and the conditions that have to exist for it to be effective, it becomes absolutely essential that you accept the premises that underlie it. Let's review what those premises are, so you can see whether you can buy into them. Then I'll proceed to a review of the technique's specific steps.

Power-Counseling Premises

First, the supervisor has an obligation to act. I believe that people do not simply respond to commands, that people sometimes need assistance and guidance and active intervention more than they need orders. This is something that the personnel department can't do, something that no one else in the organization but the supervisor can do. And if the supervisor thinks that there's a ghost of a chance of salvaging this person, if the supervisor has the willingness and the energy to try rescuing this person, then it is the supervisor's responsibility and privilege and obligation to take action and not continue avoiding the problem.

A second premise is that both people in the equation — the employee and the supervisor — need to recognize the problem for what it is and for what it is not. Problem employees do not present problems in every aspect of their behavior. They are probably on target, or at least acceptable, in many performance areas. When the supervisor counsels troubled individuals, he ought not to see them in black-and-white terms. He ought instead to see these people as having many shades in their performance, with some aspects being very acceptable and others not. It has been said that even a clock that won't run is right twice a day! Problem people are not in *all ways* a problem.

A third premise is that the supervisor's role is to help problem employees objectively perceive their own situation. The fact is that they suffer from faulty perception — they really believe that what they're doing is correct. When you listen to people who are entrenched in problem behavior, their logic is defective, and they express very defensive rationales for what they are doing. Many truly feel that their behavior is correct, acceptable, okay, justified. In fact, they don't see the situation as it really is and are deceiving themselves.

As the Scottish poet Robert Burns said:

> O wad some Pow'r the gifti gie us
> To see oursels as others see us!

The supervisor is going to give problem employees a gift — the gift being some accurate perceptions of how others are reacting to them, how the supervisor is reacting to them, and the fact that their behavior is no longer going to be tolerated or accepted and the supervisor is no longer going to avoid a confrontation.

A fourth premise that supervisors have to buy into if they're going to effectively utilize this approach is a real belief that people do not want to be judged, but rather, they want to be understood. Supervisors are called upon to be judges within the organization. They have to make judgments about people whether they like to or not. Yet, they are really trying to help problem employees understand, more than they are trying to judge them. And supervisors can only help problem employees understand by getting these employees to understand themselves first. While supervisors are certainly going to make some serious judgments about these people, their primary role is to be empathetic, not to be judgmental in what they're attempting to accomplish with them.

Finally, I believe that supervisors should undertake this technique only if they believe in human potential. Supervisors who believe that people are responsible for themselves, and that people are responsible for the choices they make in life, might want to consider using this technique. Supervisors who believe that people have the potential to work through their own problems, because they aren't the supervisors' problems but rather the employees' problems, who believe that people can choose to achieve a more effective adjustment, might want to consider using this technique.

I don't think that supervisors who don't believe in the problem employees' potential to change and to improve existing behaviors would want to utilize the power-counseling technique. On the other hand, supervisors who aren't quite ready to give up on problem employees, who believe these employees can still turn it around, who are willing to give them a last shot, and who think it's worth one final, really strong, solid, tightly organized effort on their part, might just find that this technique is for them.

The Seven Steps of Power Counseling

Frequently, I get asked: "How can I talk to somebody in a way that really penetrates the concrete? How can I get through when I know the person really doesn't want to hear me? How can I" (and the manager sometimes sounds almost desperate as he says it) "turn this person around?" Allow me to outline for you the seven-step power-counseling technique, which is based on the very positive beliefs about human potential that I've just discussed. This technique has a definite structure and a definite sequence of steps. It will not be successful with everyone, but you will achieve reasonably good success with about half of the people you try it on. And given the fact that nothing else you've tried thus far has worked, being able to turn around half of the folks at this late date may make this technique worth considering.

1. Plan Your Timing, Setting, and Opening

The first step is to consider the timing, setting, and how you're going to open this session. You should gather all the data that you can prior to the meeting. Sit down and go over your notes, pull the lost-time records if that's appropriate, visit with the personnel department, or follow whatever investigatory process will help you to really feel confident that you know what you're talking about. Do not get into a situation where you don't have all the facts. Do your homework.

When should you have this meeting with the employee? Hold the meeting as soon as possible after the employee's next deviation. His last problem behavior might have occurred months ago. It's too late now to deal with that. So wait, be prepared, and as soon as the next deviation occurs, hit the employee with it. Let's use as an example throughout this discussion the person who is a habitual latecomer or has a high rate of absenteeism. The next time this individual shows that behavior, try to confront him that same day or the next day. The point is to use the power-counseling technique when the message has the greatest chance of getting through, and that has been found to be when the occurrence is fairly recent.

Another suggestion is to try to have this conversation on a Monday, Tuesday, or Wednesday. You want to be able to see how the employee responds. If you were to have this conversation on a Friday, you might not see the employee again until Monday. On the other hand, if you talk with the person on Monday, you'll be able to see how he is doing on Tuesday and Wednesday and Thursday and Friday. So I suggest early in the week.

I also suggest having the session early in the morning or early in the shift. If you talk with the problem worker at 4:30 in the afternoon and he then goes home, you won't know how this person is doing until the next day. If you talk to the person first thing in the morning or early in the morning, you'll be able to see how he is doing throughout the afternoon. In a sense, you're going to be performing psychosurgery, and like any good surgeon, you would want to swing by the recovery room and see what shape your patient is in after the operation. You wouldn't simply go away for a week and not check the patient. So setting this up early in the day allows you the opportunity to do some follow-up monitoring afterward.

Another reason for starting early in the morning is that it is sometimes difficult to predict how long the session is going to take. If you start at 4:00 and quitting time is 5:00, but you're only halfway through with the conversation, you won't want to interrupt the process. If a patient is on the operating table and surgery is only partially completed, the doctor doesn't say, "Well it's quitting time, so I'm going to knock off now and head for home." Once you start the power-counseling session, you must see it through to the end.

The setting must be private. The employee has to receive your undivided attention during a very serious conversation. If your office has windows in it, then go to an office that doesn't have windows. If you have to, paper up your windows! This session should not be subject to any interruptions. And that means that you will have arranged for somebody to take your calls. It means that you will have arranged for somebody to handle emergencies. In fact, nothing will be more important than completing this conversation. You may want to tip off your boss that you are going to be in this conference. If it looks as if you're going to be getting close to lunch hour, then have an understanding with the person before you start that the conference may extend through the lunch hour, so there aren't any false expectations.

How long will the session take? My experience is that you can typically count on an hour to an hour and a half. Even so, I would recommend allowing three hours in your schedule. Give yourself ample time for the conversation to run beyond its expected length, and do not schedule any appointments immediately around this conference.

You want to project a very serious image as the person comes into your office. He may be joking, complaining about the weather, or commenting on Monday night football, but my suggestion is not to respond to any social conversation. You and this employee aren't here to chat about the weather or about any of the fun things in life. You are both here because there is an extremely serious problem. You need to send a message that will help the employee understand that you are dead serious about his current performance.

There are a number of things you can do that will help you set a tone of seriousness. First, dress like an undertaker: dark blue, dark black, or dark brown suit; white shirt; no flashy jewelry or ornamentation. This is not the day to wear your Hawaiian shirt to the office. This is a day in which to look like an authority figure. This is a day in which you will want to send other signals that will help the employee grasp what's going on. I suggest that you arrange your office so that you sit on one side of the desk and the employee sits on the other. You should not be sitting side by side like chums on the couch. This is not a transactional analysis or human relations course; this is a tough talk between a boss and a person who has placed himself outside the accepted range of behavior.

Give some special consideration to the chair that the employee will sit in. Do not give him a soft, overstuffed easy chair that's very comfortable. The employee shouldn't feel comfortable in this environment. After all, were you comfortable in planning for it? The employee needs to feel discomfort because that will help him understand the seriousness of the offense. A number of managers have reported good success using very hard chairs. Think of the most uncomfortable chair imaginable, and that is the chair to use. Do not use a chair with arms. There should be as little support and as little comfort in the chair as possible. In fact, this is the hot seat.

Think about the way in which a court sends a message to people who are in violation of society's standards. In a typical courtroom, the judge's bench is in fact nothing but a very big desk, raised on a dais to emphasize his authority. The judge wears special attire—a dark suit or robes. The judge's clothing is symbolic of his power and the seriousness of the moment. When brought before the bar, the prisoner is not made comfortable. The judge, through the trappings of his office, sends a very powerful message: "You had better listen to what I'm about to tell you."

If you start off the conference with your problem person in some other way— wearing your T-shirt that says you're a member of the Pepsi generation, seating the employee in a comfy chair, and chatting amiably about the ball game—the tone is going to be out of sync when you then bring up the topic of performance deficiencies and discrepancies. It is simply more honest and consistent to tip the employee off at the outset that this is serious. By your dress and demeanor, you send a message that the employee can pick up on and thereby realize, "Uh oh, I'm in trouble."

While every manager who uses this technique has to adapt it to his own personality, and modify it to fit his situation, the common picture at this point is one of a manager's being very firm, direct, purposeful, and straight to the point. The employee may enter the office chatting in an animated manner. Silence him and say, "Please sit in that chair." Some managers will even point to the chair with the air of an authority figure as they say this. To start off the conversation, some managers will say: "We're not here to talk about the weather. We have something far more important to discuss."

Again, this is partly a matter of style. But whatever the manager's style, I want to stress that he must *communicate effectively* right now. Effectiveness in communication does not necessarily mean softness, gentleness, or happiness. Chris Argyris, one of America's greatest experts on attitude and behavior change, has said that when trying to change people's attitudes, you must realize that they have to go through an unfreezing process—that is, there has to be a thawing of the very fixed, set opinions they now have. If the task were to melt ice, we would all know what to do: Apply some heat. So turn up the heat to cause melting. When you've broken through these very fixed defensive positions and rationalizations the employee has erected around his inappropriate behavior, only then will the employee be able to consider new behavior possibilities. The manager's job is to help with the unfreezing process and then provide new direction, learning opportunity, and some help as the employee comes to his or her own conclusions about what needs to be done. And then, Argyris said, the person's opinions will refreeze, hopefully in a better arrangement than they were before.

As the manager begins, he is very distant. To the employee, the manager probably appears cold, remote, threatening, and intimidating. And yet, in the course of the seven steps, the manager will move from this very distant position to a very close position. A transition will occur from negative to positive, but the process begins on a negative note. To continue the surgery analogy, the operation begins with some cutting and some removal of tissue. Later there will be stitching and the application of ointments and bandages and the start of the healing process. The surgeon knows this is a condition that is not going to be cured simply by kissing it to make it all better. The problem employee situation is no different. It is going to require some surgery, some excision of the employee's inappropriate behavior. So there will be some negative, distant feelings at the start of the conversation. But we are progressing through a counseling that will eventually get us to those positive, close feelings.

One last recommendation regarding the opening is to concentrate on present behavior and not on past history. What a person has done in the last six years is not immediately relevant. What to deal with now are current infractions, the most recent tardiness. One of the reasons for picking the most recent occurrence is that it will certainly be clearest in people's minds and least subject to memory distortions attributable to the passage of time. In addition to absenteeism, there may be 47 other things wrong with this employee, but in this case, deal only with one, two, or at most, three problem behaviors. The power-counseling technique cannot remake this person into a perfect individual. So deal with recent events and deal with a limited but carefully chosen list of behaviors.

2. Send the Confrontation Message

The second step of the power-counseling process is to present the direct confrontation message to the employee. The confrontation message is comprised of three parts. The first part involves giving specific information and includes the following five elements:

1. A statement of what the policy is
2. What all employees should do in light of that policy
3. The facts of the employee's own particular behavior
4. Whose fault the deviation is
5. The problems that it's creating

A specific message to the latecomer could go like this:

Tom, our policy is that all employees should report to work on time. It's the practice of every employee in the unit to come on time. Under our compensation procedures, we pay people for their hours or for their adherence to other kinds of standards. In your case, company practice requires that you be here on time each and every morning. Therefore, like every other employee, you should do that. You've got to live up to that policy and practice. It's simply the way we do things around here, and the fact is that your tardiness is at variance with that, and it has now become a serious issue.

We've had repeated conversations about this; yet you were late again yesterday morning. You're responsible for your latecoming; it's your problem. And this deviation is not acceptable around here. It's causing a great deal of friction, it's creating dissension among the group, it's creating personal frustration on my part, and I don't like it.

The second part of the confrontation is to deliver the actual confrontation message. While there's a lot of room for variation and individual interpretation in the counseling process, I would suggest that you consider using verbatim the following three-sentence message:

I will no longer tolerate _____ in your behavior. Effective _____, I expect you to stop _____. I also expect that by _____ [again mention the date], you will change your behavior to _____.

In the case of our latecomer, the dialog would look like this:

I will no longer tolerate *latecoming* in your behavior. Effective *immediately,* I expect you to stop *your tardiness.* I also expect that *immediately* you will change your behavior to *coming to work on time each and every day.*

If you analyze what is being said in those three sentences, you'll notice several important points. First, the message is communicated efficiently, because in three sentences, you mention twice what it is you're not going to tolerate. You mention twice what the deadline is by which the employee must change, and you also mention what the expected new behavior is. Something else is contained in those sentences: your position statement, in which you say, "I will no longer tolerate. . . ." That means you are at the end of the road — a clear and up-front message that can't be ignored by the employee.

Give some consideration to how you will convey this message. I think it should be delivered with some drama or some impact. Some managers will raise their voice when delivering the message. Others will speak their piece very softly or very slowly.

However you deliver the message, say it in some form or fashion that will reach this person. It is very clear at this point in your relationship with him that nothing has been getting through. Find some way to dramatize your message or multiply its impact. One manager reports that he not only delivers his message slowly, but he writes out each word as he says it! He gears his speaking speed to his writing speed and writes out the message about what it is he's no longer going to tolerate and then hands it to the employee.

At this point in the conversation, you've said what the policy is and that the employee isn't adhering to it even though he should be. You've said it's the employee's fault and that he is causing friction and frustration. And finally, you've said: "I'm not going to tolerate it. I expect you to stop it and start doing something better."

Dealing with Interruptions

Just about now, you're going to get a reaction from the problem employee. The employee is either going to rise up out of the chair and want to speak or won't even have allowed you to get this far. In the event that you are interrupted prior to finishing the confrontation message, don't permit the employee to speak. Interrupt his interruption by saying, "Please allow me to continue," or say "Please allow me to finish." Most people will back off and let you do that.

One of the reasons for insisting on getting your message out is that at this stage, you're still playing the power and judgment role with the employee. By forcing him to comply with the modest request of hearing you out, you're setting a pattern and tone of getting the employee to adhere to the line and direction you set. But another reason that you're not going to let this person interrupt your message is because he may say something stupid. The fact is, the employee has only heard two parts of the message at this point. The third part is still to come. And when the employee experiences this initial attack and confrontation he will react very defensively and want to respond to what you're saying. In so doing, the employee is going to embarrass himself. You know where this process is heading, but the employee doesn't. So in order to protect his interests, state it as clearly as this, if necessary:

> Listen, I'm going to finish talking, and then it will be your turn. Please do me the courtesy of listening to me first, and then I'll listen to you.

Under no circumstances should you let this break down into a discussion. Do not let the employee interrupt you during the second part of the confrontation message.

The third part of the confrontation message is to express confidence in the employee. After you have told him what the policy and practice are, and gone over the employee's failings, what the facts are, and the frustration the behavior is causing, and after you have delivered to him the direct three-sentence confrontation message, there is one other message you must deliver. You must express your belief that the employee can achieve the required changes and indicate that you are trying to help. Some managers state it like this:

> You know, we wouldn't be having this talk at all if I didn't believe in you. Given your capabilities and what I believe your potential to be, I'm amazed we're even having this discussion.

> This problem is so far beneath you that I don't understand how you can put up with it. I'm here to help you, but you've got to make this change on your own.

That is the first positive message the employee has received in an otherwise alarming first few moments of the counseling session. When the employee hears on the one hand that you are coming down hard on an aspect of his behavior, but hears on the other hand an expression of positive beliefs and a statement that you're there offering help and support, then that changes your posture in his eyes. You become less an enemy and more a parental figure, more a counselor, and that's a different kind of role. It's a distinct difference, and it will tend to temper the employee's response to you subsequently. Once the employee has the idea that you have not closed him out, then this individual may remain open to the process that you're trying to utilize. And that is the goal here.

Another possible reaction you should be prepared for, either at this point or a little earlier in the conversation, is that the employee may say, "Well if you feel that way, and you find my behavior so unacceptable, why don't you fire me?" Beware, because this question is designed to test your resolve. If you panic and hurry to reassure the employee by saying, "Oh, we're not here for me to fire you. We're just here to have this talk," then the employee will figure that you're not serious and that he can continue to get away with it.

At this critical juncture, go back to your own words and consider their import — "I will no longer tolerate this in your behavior." What you said in that declaration was that this is the end of the road and that the person must now comply or be gone. So when asked about your readiness to fire the problem worker, you can respond by saying:

> At the moment, we're not here to discuss your termination. We're here to talk about your willingness to change your behavior.

Or:

> I suppose we could discuss termination if you like, but I called you into my office this morning to see whether you can do something to change your behavior, so we won't have to talk about your leaving the company.

Say it however you want to, but let the message be clearly understood in the employee's mind that you have drawn your sword and that if he wants you to use it, you will. But also let the employee understand that while your hand rests on the sword's hilt, you have not yet decided to lay the weapon across the back of his neck. In this way, the employee knows that "the ruler" is ready to take action, if required, but is giving "the subject" one last chance to comply. I think it's very important that the employee sense no weakness or lack of resolve in your manner. He must understand very clearly that you mean exactly what you have said. *You will no longer tolerate it.*

3. Hear Out the Employee's Facts, Fictions, and Faking

The third step in this counseling process is the ventilation of all the employee's excuses and reasons why he has been misbehaving. You are going to hear a stream of "facts" as the employee sees them, and a lot of fictions, faking, and preliminary dancing around the central issue of what is really going on.

Some of the things you're going to hear are projections of blame onto you: You never provided him with the training, you never explained it that way before, you never did this, you never did that. And there is a possibility that the employee may get you on one or two of those charges. You may not have performed your job perfectly. You may have failed to do some things that probably you should have done. But even though the employee may have caught you in some kind of managerial shortcoming, do not buy into guilt. What the employee is trying to do is take the monkey off his back and put it on yours. If you can be persuaded that the employee's failure is your fault, then that gets him or her off the hook. So simply respond:

> We're not here to talk about my failings or the failings that you think I have. We're here to talk about your responsibility to comply with the policy that all employees have to abide by.

Later that night you may want to reflect long and hard on some of the things you failed to do this time that you won't fail to do next time. But don't buy into any guilt for taking action with this employee.

Your purpose at this stage is to let the employee do nearly all the talking. He should be talking 95 percent of the time right now. What you're going to hear are referred to as defense mechanisms. People under attack always maintain their innocence.

The defense mechanisms include such tactics as the employee making excuses for his behavior. Whatever he might have done, you can bet that the employee has rationalized it in great detail. You will also hear projections of blame — that it was your fault or another employee's fault. You will be treated to tales of hard times growing up in the ghetto, troubles with the neighbors, or problems in the family. You're going to hear partial truths, fantasy, and selective reporting.

During this outpouring, your only response should be to encourage its flow. You should be saying: "Uh-huh. Yes. I see. Then what happened? Tell me more. Go on." Inwardly, you may be thinking, "This has got to be the biggest bunch of baloney I've ever heard in my life." Your role right now, however, is to be the listener.

Just by listening, you are sending an important signal. To listen and nod and ask for more information is the behavior of a person who is on the employee's side. You may be mentally rejecting much of what you're hearing. And in fact, a lot of the stuff employees come out with at this point is absolute nonsense or complete falsity. But in the midst of this flood of excuses will be bits and pieces of truth — information that you may have been unaware of or that does start to give you some insights. What has to be recognized is that you have started a catharsis. Around his problem behavior, the employee has erected high protective walls comprised of all kinds of excuses. Those walls must be dismantled. In a sense, it's almost as if an emotional storm or a psychological drainage were occurring. Until that storm dissipates, until that emotion and anger drain out of the system, you cannot get the employee to the point of being able to deal with the problem in a constructive way.

Some managers don't understand this process. They think that because the employee is giving out partial information or rationalizing, he isn't dealing with the issue. In fact, the employee is dealing with it, but this first level of dealing with it is being expressed through these defense mechanisms.

If you become sidetracked and get drawn into a discussion of any one of the points that the employee raises at this stage, you'll be making a big mistake. Say to yourself as you go into the third stage: "I am not going to respond except to encourage this person to talk. And if he says such and such about so and so, I am not going to get sidetracked or say, 'Yeah, well prove it,' or, 'Where's the evidence for that?' or, 'Let's discuss that point.' " Don't get sidetracked. It will be absolutely counterproductive. If you can see this process through the eyes of a professional psychologist and observe it in an almost clinical way, you will understand that defense mechanisms are the best way in which a struggling human being can deal with this sort of tough situation.

Some managers have a difficult time accepting defensive reactions. Maybe people shouldn't be like this. Maybe they should just be able to deal rationally with all their problems and never hide some of the real reasons for their behavior. Maybe they ought to be that way, but they're not. Effective managers are pragmatists; they're realists. They deal with people the way they are and concede that defensive reactions are just normal behavior. Maybe to you, defensive reactions seem reprehensible, not quite moral or ethical. If you can, avoid making judgments and simply play the role of a detached spectator, observing an interesting behavioral phenomenon.

What you're seeing at this stage is sometimes characterized by people in the counseling game as a lot of "psychological vomit," to use their indelicate but apt term. When you're really sick to your stomach, sometimes the only way you're going to feel better is to get rid of what's bothering you. And that's what's occurring in step three.

Sometimes what prevents people from getting down to business isn't anything as psychologically involved or as elegant-sounding as defense mechanisms. Sometimes there is simple embarrassment. Sometimes you'll encounter a person who just has a very hard time with words and cannot express himself very clearly. Sometimes people don't understand themselves very well and have such faulty perceptions that they're really hemmed in. Again, the key behavior on your part: Hear the person out, encourage the flow, and finally, listen for the sigh.

Getting the Most Out of Step Three

What is the sigh? The sigh is the sound you're going to hear when a person reaches the end of step three. Initially, the employee's conversation is going to run pretty much nonstop. There'll be a lot of very rapid conversation, an unbroken flow of words and stories. And then the employee is going to pause, reach an end point, and sigh. The sigh is a signal, a cue, that he is beginning to relax and that the venting process is probably getting close to completion. Other signals you can look for are a settling back in the chair, a slumping down of the shoulders, or a general relaxing of body tension. The employee sometimes even expresses it verbally: "Well, I guess that's about all I have to say."

Step three certainly illustrates my communication rule that "Whatever I say it is, it isn't." We are so clever that we often do not express things the way they really are. We use misleading labels and invent excuses. We're so skilled in communicating that we know how to miscommunicate. Remember the second of Sherman's rules of communication: "Whatever I say it is, there is always more." And when you hear the sigh, when the employee falls silent, do not assume that's all there is. There's always more.

There are a number of ways to encourage the employee to provide additional information that he might not have revealed yet. One is to simply remain silent. Your silence invites the employee to say something to you—almost forces him to do so, in fact. Another way to deal with the end of step three is to give the employee some encouragement:

I certainly have been impressed by your willingness to share this with me. I think you've really tried to give me a picture of what the situation is. Is there anything else you'd like to say?

Giving the employee a positive stroke, followed by an invitation to say something more, is sometimes enough to prompt him to resume talking. Keep questioning and keep listening attentively. Often what people say at the very end of the conversation is some of the most important information a manager gets. So if you can give the person two or three more chances past where you sense the normal end point would be, you'll sometimes uncover some additional useful information.

Through all of this, you will have heard many very interesting things that should enable you to make some preliminary judgments about how well the employee understands what the real world is like. You may have discovered some internal conflicts. You may have found out about some needs. You may have gotten a different picture of this person or sensed some of the pressures that he is responding to. You may learn something about expectations the employee has that haven't been met, which could explain why he is passively resisting by coming in late. You will start to get a sense of what is going on with this person. And my final point is that until this venting has occurred, he will be unable to proceed to the next step in the power-counseling process.

4. Define the Problem and Formulate Options

The purpose of step four is to help the employee better define the problem and to start formulating some answers and options. As you move from distance to closeness, from pain to healing with positive behavior, step four brings another opportunity in the interview where you can begin to signal to the employee that he is indeed making some progress.

I would recommend that you now invite the employee to bring his chair around to the side of your desk so that the two of you can start writing some things down on paper and looking at the elements of the problem. You should not move your chair to be closer to the employee because you're correctly positioned. The employee is the one out of position. The employee is the one who removed himself from the straight and narrow path. By having the employee get up and move his chair to the side of your desk, you are symbolizing a move closer to you and to corporate standards. You're not yet totally together, but you're closer, and what brings you closer is step four, which allows the employee to work on options for solution.

A useful technique at this point in the session is to ask the employee to summarize in writing the factors that he feels have contributed to the problem. The purpose of trying to put this on paper is that it reduces the interpersonal tension between the two parties and focuses mutual attention on the factors of the problem that are written on the piece of paper. If you're dealing with a very sophisticated employee, you might ask him not only to list the factors but to rank-order them. If you're dealing with an employee who is barely literate, then you might want to serve as the secretary and write the factors down. In any event, it is important that you not provide any input to the list on the paper but rather ask questions of the employee until he verbalizes what contributed to the

problem. If this is not done, and you insist on putting down your version of what's involved in the problem, it then becomes your list, not the employee's.

As the employee lists factors that he thought contributed to the problem, some elements will be put down that may not really be part of the problem. Don't be upset at this. In a sense, it's as if the employee were setting up pins in a bowling alley. As the manager listens to the various reasons for why Tom is late — which might include his broken car, the alarm clock that didn't go off, or the fight he had with his wife the night before — it becomes apparent that some of those elements were probably major contributing factors and others were not. The key at this point is not to get into an argument or discussion about the contributing factors that the manager doesn't agree to. Rather, when the list is complete, the manager can simply say: "You know, Tom, I really agree with items three, six, and eight. It just seems to me that those really stand out as the primary factors in the problem." If the employee has set up the bowling pins, the manager, in confirming certain points, is rolling the ball down the alley and hitting those pins that he agrees with.

It's important to remember the objective here — that the manager reach some kind of agreement with the employee regarding what the problem is and that it be an agreement that the employee will buy into. The employee does not have to see the situation entirely through the manager's eyes, as long as they are in agreement on the key elements.

Sometimes managers ask why they should bother having the employee write down the elements. The purpose is to get this information out of the employee's head and down on paper, thereby reducing the emotion and improving the communication dynamics. Usually, these matters are difficult to talk about, with many factors and considerable emotion involved. Putting it on paper allows both parties to the conversation to distance themselves from the emotion, and it forces them to verbalize in a more objective way what is going on. The act of writing down the problem's elements changes the tone of the discussion between the manager and the employee. Before, the two parties looked directly at each other and interpreted the messages personally across a desk. But putting the issues on paper makes the two parties look not at each other in a challenging way but at the document, side by side, in a problem-solving way. This simple technique really reduces the tension in the situation.

At this stage of defining and clarifying the problem in writing, the manager should be asking a lot of questions. Appropriate questions might be:

- Tom, you didn't used to be late so often. What change in your situation has caused this to become a problem now?
- Tom, does your not coming in on time indicate that you don't want to be here at work?
- Are you still satisfied with your work assignments? Do you still like your job?

What the manager is attempting to do is help the employee gain some insight and self understanding. The question stream from the manager also gives him a much better view of the employee's perceptions and where the employee has been deceiving himself about this situation. So ask as many questions as make sense. Even write down a couple of pages' worth beforehand if that will help.

There is one specific question that should definitely be asked toward the end of this step: "Tom, what do you think your future is going to be if you continue to come in late?" In this question, you're asking Tom to predict his future, and the usual response will be along the lines of "Well, I guess I could be fired." When that is said—and it usually will be—the employee has demonstrated a good appreciation of exactly where he stands in the relationship. The manager should then confirm that understanding. "Yes, Tom, I think I would have no other choice but to terminate you if this tardiness continues."

On the other hand, the employee still may not quite understand, or grasp the seriousness of the moment, and say, "I guess I don't know what you mean." At this point the manager should realize that the person may be even more difficult to reach than he seemed at first, and so the manager will again have to spell out that he is not going to tolerate the behavior anymore and that if it continues, the employee will have to be terminated. The purpose of this test question is to confirm whether the employee is with you in terms of understanding the potential consequences.

A second question that I would ask immediately after that test question is: "Tom, what solutions can you come up with that will change that outcome? What can you do to keep that prediction from coming true?" If he's with it, Tom will say, "We've been working on this list, and I guess if I get items three, six, and eight, that might really take some of the pressure off." By so saying, Tom is indicating his understanding of the conversation. This positive response deserves confirmation: "Yes, Tom, I think that would go a long way toward solving my concerns."

Again, if the employee just cannot figure out what has to be done in order to make this problem go away, here's another chance for the supervisor to spell it out: "Here are the items you put on your list, and if you don't correct these matters, if you don't get yourself to work on time and improve your commitment and your attitude about getting to work on time, then this is what's going to happen."

5. Reach Agreement

Step five in the process is to reach an agreement on the solution. In the previous step, there was a fairly rational discussion in which the factors were laid out and predictions were made about what would happen if that plan were not adhered to. Even though a general understanding was reached in that discussion, the manager should not assume there is an agreement.

At this point, another document should be drawn up—what I would term a performance contract. That contract should be written by the employee, or by the manager if he is acting as the scribe. It should spell out exactly what the employee is going to do; how, when, where, and with whom he is going to do it; and what the standards of performance will be. With Tom's tardiness problem, the statement might be quite simple:

> I will come to work on time each and every morning from this date forward. To help me do that, I'm going to get the supportive tools I need: a new alarm clock and a more

reliable ride to work. Also I'm going to just get with the idea of coming to work on time.

I will see my manager every morning when I come in so there's no question that I was here on time.

The last item in that sample performance contract established the review schedule. This provides an opportunity for the manager to monitor progress toward the new behavior. As a rule, I would make progress-review points quite frequent. At a later time, as the employee seems to be getting on track, the manager can back off the review frequency and let Tom come to see him on Monday, Wednesday, and Friday mornings. The very act of lessening the frequency with which review is going to take place sends very positive messages to the employee — but that should be saved for later.

The performance contract should then be signed and dated by both parties. On the positive side, what you're doing is trying to be very clear in your instructions to the employee and getting the employee to put in writing what all his thinking and discussion have been about. Doing so has been found to help people in changing their behavior.

On the negative side, if the employee does not honor the contract in the future, you have grounds for dismissal. Since you indicated that you were no longer going to tolerate this behavior, and since you have a signed and dated statement saying that as of this point forward, the employee was going to change his behavior, if the contract is now violated, you have sufficient basis for termination.

What if the employee doesn't want to sign the performance contract? At that point, I would call a third party into the office, explain to him what has been discussed, and indicate that the employee does not want to sign the agreement. Then ask the offending employee again if he wouldn't like to sign the agreement pledging themself to acceptable behavior. After you have given the employee a second chance, if he still does not sign the performance contract, then the third party should sign it as a witness that the employee was asked to sign this statement but refused.

Should the employee be fired for not signing the document? No. The employee wrote that he would live up to the standard but simply refused to sign the paper. If the employee comes to work every day thereafter on time, that is the only compliance the manager really cares about. The purpose of getting the employee to sign is to help him make a commitment, but the act of not signing doesn't by itself mean that the employee won't commit. Nevertheless, to protect yourself legally, have the refusal to sign witnessed.

I think the attitude and tone surrounding the creation of the performance contract should not reflect legal formalities so much as the goal of helpful and clear communication. I think the attitude that the manager should display is reflected in the following statement:

> Tom, I just want to be sure that both of us have a crystal-clear understanding. This matter is too important for there to be any misunderstanding between us later on. You've put in some real effort to come up with a workable plan. I want us both to recognize that it's a workable plan, and let's really make a commitment to it. I'd like you to sign it, and I'm going to do the same. And we'll both keep a copy, so there won't be any confusion afterward.

In many cases, employees report that when they were in hot water like this, such an approach was helpful to them. It assured them that as long as they lived up to their part of the bargain, they would be okay. The agreement wasn't going to be subject to any whimsical changes on the part of the manager. So the performance contract can be presented and used as a very positive thing.

6. Get Commitment

The sixth step is to go beyond the written statement outlining the solution, which forms the basis of the performance contract, and ask the employee for a commitment and a promise. A number of commitments are really being made here. The first is the direct request to the employee to commit to the stated behavior change: "Tom, will you do this?" Through sad experience, I've learned that you cannot assume that an employee will do it even though he has written and signed a performance contract. By asking for a verbal commitment, you may get a better indication of what the person's behavior is actually going to be. If Tom says, "No, I won't do it," I would admire Tom's honesty and respect his integrity, in that he has been up-front about that.

But if Tom does indicate that he isn't going to change, then your next step would be to proceed immediately with termination. You put yourself on record at the beginning of the conversation as saying that you were no longer going to tolerate this behavior, and Tom has now honestly reported that he won't change. The only option remaining to the supervisor is termination. So take the necessary steps in order to bring the relationship to a close as quickly and neatly as possible.

On the other hand, assuming Tom has really sensed that you believe in him, and assuming Tom has something in him that makes him want to improve, he may respond by saying yes. If he does say yes, it doesn't necessarily mean that he actually will improve his behavior. But most of those who say they will, make a very solid effort at doing so. There will, of course, be a group of people who say they'll shape up but won't. There will be those who won't live up to their performance contract and won't reveal that to you during the conversation but will reveal it by their behavior the following morning, and these individuals should then be terminated, as well.

Just as the employee commits to making an effort, some unspoken commitments have to be made by the manager, too. I think the manager at this point has to commit within himself to provide Tom with continued communication, coaching, and counseling, together with training and other assistance that may be helpful. A good deal of management support will be necessary as the employee now struggles to improve. You don't simply say, "Now that you're in the pool, sink or swim." The manager instead has to make a commitment to stand by and work with the employee.

A common experience of managers who go through this process is that they learn about things that are wrong within their own department or organization. They find out about factors that are acting as negative influences on the employee. And that means the manager now has to go to work and fight city hall and change the procedures and deal with some of these conditions that are holding Tom back. The manager's own hands may be entirely clean, but very often these cases involve a mixed bag of factors. Some elements, perhaps most, belong in the employee's area of responsibility, but other elements may suggest that the manager needs to clean up the operating environment within which that employee works.

7. Close with Healing

Step seven is to wrap up the conference. You've moved a long way — from looking like a judge and acting like an executioner, down through an emotional venting process, on to the creation of a tentative work plan, and finally to a written performance contract backed up by a verbal commitment. And if successful, you've moved a failing human being back onto the track of acceptable performance. What a great achievement!

As you moved through the conversation, the balance shifted. This is a human being who is now working with you, who is developing a performance contract and making a commitment to do better. This employee needs and deserves something from you. It's been a painful one- or two-hour conversation; yet, it's been good, too, because a lot has been accomplished. So how do you wrap this up? You should give some serious thought to how you want to do that.

This certainly isn't going to be a perfect person when you're done with this performance-counseling session. There may be a number of other things that he needs to work on, and perhaps there'll be future sessions like this one to deal with other problems. But people generally change more readily when they have a sense of confidence about the change, a positive feeling, and certainly they'll be far more inclined to make the changes you want if they leave your office filled with hope than if they leave filled with fear and anxiety and feeling threatened.

To end the conversation, stand up. Since you are the authority figure, the other person will also automatically stand. You now have an opportunity to bridge the last physical distance remaining between the two of you. The employee has been sitting at the side of your desk, and you can now reach out and shake his hand. I suggest that you carefully consider just how you're going to do the handshake. I think a firm or prolonged handshake is called for. Some managers report that they use a two-handed handshake. As you grip the hand, give a very brief message:

> I realize this has been a tough discussion, but it's been a productive discussion, too. I like the attitude and the commitment that you've shown here. I said to you at the very beginning that we wouldn't be having this talk at all if I didn't think you had the capability to improve your performance. I'm confident that you've got what it takes and that you're going to deal with this. I want you to know I'm counting on you.

To that central concept can be added any other message that you'd like to deliver. Generally, what's called for is a brief, supportive statement clearly indicating that you support the employee as much as you oppose the negative behavior that he has shown.

Some managers, when they conclude the message and have hold of the employee with both hands, pull the employee off balance toward them. This body language, in which the manager literally tugs the employee in his direction, can be very effective in sending the message that, now that the employee has come a long way toward the manager, the manager is going to actively pull the employee even closer — closer to the manager and closer to the path of acceptable performance. In these days of sexual harassment suits, I think you have to consider the touch question carefully. Some managers say that knowing their people and their personalities, it seems natural just to touch them lightly on the shoulder with their hand as the employees go out the door. Other male managers, particularly with male employees, will sometimes use a closed fist to lightly tap the employee on the shoulder, with the message, "Go get 'em, Tiger!" That's body language that many boys picked up from a father or coach. You have to use some judgment and discretion here. Generally, the handshake is always safe, and anything else that implies a closeness that is not offensive would be appropriate.

The value in touch is that it evokes a very human response. Having been through an emotional, difficult, and demanding experience, the employee knows that he has really blown it in the eyes of the boss. For the boss to then reach out like this signals in a far more powerful way than words could possibly express that the employee has not been shut out. It's not uncommon to even get a tear or two from the employee at this point, as the employee comes to realize that you're still in touch with him. What you're attempting to communicate in the closing is that you aren't trying to shut out the employee, you don't have a vendetta against the employee, and you aren't trying to railroad the employee or run him out of town on a rail. You are simply insisting that some negative behavior has to stop and some positive behavior has to start.

I think the other element of the closure, at least on the day of the performance-counseling session, is to be sure to swing by that employee's office or work station later, talk to him normally, and make no reference to the earlier conversation. A very powerful thing to do at that point might be to give the employee a piece of work and say, "Would you please look into this and handle it." Assigning work to an employee at this time is basically a message of trust: "I still trust you to handle responsibility. I'm not going to clam up or give you the silent treatment. I'm not going to pout when I walk by. I'm not going to frown at you."

The intent of this communication later in the day is to let the employee know that bygones are bygones: "Today we have work to do, and there are things I want to chat with you about." You have to send a message that says, "It's over now, and I'm not going to be running around here checking up on you, carrying a grudge, or acting negatively or suspiciously toward you." If the employee senses normalcy from you, I think it will go a long way toward normalizing the relationship.

Summary

Power counseling is a seven-step approach to conducting a last-ditch shape-up-or-ship-out discussion with a problem employee regarding his behavior or performance.

The process begins with preparation, as the manager plans the timing and setting of the counseling session and decides on how to handle its opening. The second step is for the manager to deliver to the employee a three-part confrontation message, which (1) conveys information about the problem performance or behavior, (2) indicates that the manager will no longer tolerate the situation and expects to see a very prompt improvement, and (3) expresses the manager's confidence in the employee's ability to turn the situation around.

Now that the manager has delivered his basic message, the next step is for the manager to hear the employee out. This will often involve listening attentively to assorted excuses, fault finding and finger pointing, partial truths and outright lies. In the course of this outpouring, certain legitimate facts will emerge, and the manager will gain some valuable insights into the employee and his behavior. The act of listening itself also enables the manager to demonstrate respect for the employee and begin to establish a connection with him.

Once the manager has confirmed that the employee has indeed fully expressed his side of the story, the power-counseling process moves on to defining the problem — in writing — and developing options for correcting it. The written approach to problem definition and option formulation can take the focus off the interpersonal manager-employee confrontation and turn the session into one in which the manager and the employee are on the same side, jointly confronting the performance problem and working together to develop a solution.

After the options for solution have been identified, the manager and the employee draw up a written performance contract, detailing the improved behavior or performance to which the employee pledges himself and the schedule for the manager's review of the employee's progress. The manager asks, too, for an oral confirmation of the employee's commitment to the change effort — a spoken promise to improve. The manager at this point also commits himself to taking whatever measures may be necessary to support the employee's change effort.

The manager wraps up the power-counseling session by decisively starting the healing process — restating his confidence in the employee's ability to get back on track and confirming this physically, with a warm handshake or some other appropriate, supportive touch. The message of reconciliation is reinforced when, later in the day, the manager stops by the employee's work station to reestablish a tone of normalcy in the working relationship.

Remember, this counseling technique is powerful. Don't use it if you don't accept and believe deeply in the premises on which it is based. It requires some preplanning and perhaps even some rehearsal. It works best when the manager takes a detached, clinical stance. It is essential for the manager to keep the process on track, yet give each stage the time and emphasis it requires. And it just may help the manager get through to people who are worth saving.

12

Fire Somebody

Terminating an employee is the toughest task in management, and managers shrink from doing it—in fact, almost refuse to do it. As a consultant, I've worked with more than a thousand organizations across North America and Europe. Almost without exception, I hear the stories of supervisors who express their desire to fire someone but just can't get up the nerve to do so. It's important to understand the psychological dynamics of that management resistance. Managers resist firing people for some very positive reasons as well as for some that aren't so laudatory.

Why Managers Don't Fire People

First, let's remember that managers are a different breed. As individuals, they typically have risen to a high level in their profession, have proved themselves through long years of study or experience, and like to do things right. They have a high need for achievement. The surest way to frustrate them is to prevent their attaining a goal. The major reason why managers don't fire people is because they refuse to give up on another person. The managers may be absolutely upset and unhappy at having to confront the problem worker every day, and yet, deep down, there is a dynamic operating that says, "I cannot admit defeat with this person."

In part, I believe that dynamic is extremely helpful. I recall the people in my own life who helped turn me around. Think of the people who were instrumental in shaping your life. Others may have felt inclined to give up on you, but these folks didn't. And because they didn't, because they stuck with you, they got a transformation—they set you on a new track.

Professional sports offer many examples of people who left one team in failure, as losers. But they went on to join another team and performed with such excellence that they were voted into the hall of fame. The difference in the equation was a coach who believed in them, who stuck with them. And what leadership has to do sometimes, when an individual is seen wrestling with a poor-performance problem, is to stick with the person during that period. When I see a manager who knows he probably ought to fire an employee and yet refuses to do it, what I am often seeing is a high achiever who just won't give up.

But there's a negative side to this picture — or at least the possibility of a negative side — and that is that sometimes the high achiever fails to recognize that there are some things he cannot accomplish. In certain cases, the high achiever does not want to be seen politically as being unable to handle all of the problems within his unit. This type of individual can be such a perfectionist that, perhaps out of fear of failure, he sometimes has inordinate difficulty in coming to grips with hopeless situations. The high achiever fights on and resists terminating the employee, fearing to be seen as a loser.

To the perfectionists among you, let me offer this counsel. The coaches whose teams win most often in sports, the executives who are most effective in organizations, are those who know when the time has come to cut a nonproducer. If you really want to excel, you must face the fact that you cannot win with losers. While your own skills at turning people around may be substantial, there are some people you will not succeed in reaching. To really be a winner in management means that you have to be sufficiently objective. Objectivity must not be confused with pessimism; rather, it is an honest recognition that you are going to win some and lose some. Babe Ruth did not bat a thousand, Tom Landry did not win every game, not every composition by Bach was great, nor will you save every problem employee.

So while I respect your unwillingness to make termination your first option for managing people, and I respect your sticking with a person whom you're trying to turn around, I do not respect the manager who fails to recognize that there comes a time when you have to move on to other approaches and to other people. The work of your profession, the mission of your organization, is too important to be sacrificed to a stubborn resistance to taking action when it is clearly called for.

Another major reason why managers don't fire people stems from their own anxiety and uncertainty about how to do it. The reality is that this is an infrequently performed function, the skills that are required to do it are not used every day, and so there is some performance anxiety: "Will I handle it correctly?" There is also some anxiety about potential legal action — about managerial missteps that might later haunt the company in court.

Still another powerful reason why managers refuse to fire is a humanistic concern about what will happen to this person. No one deliberately wants to hurt another, and the idea that the job requires the manager to make a judgment about this person that will necessitate his termination means that the manager is going to inflict pain on that person and create difficulty in his life. Managers facing this task will talk about the other person's family, children, mortgage, and so on.

A Philosophy of Firing

To managers who have difficulty firing problem employees who deserve termination, I offer Sherman's law:

Fire people so that they can be
successful someplace else.

While that strikes some people as an astonishing statement, think about what is happening to people who are in jeopardy of termination. They know they're not performing well. They know they're not meeting expectations. Every morning as they get up, they know they're about to go to a job where their boss has largely rejected them. They may be facing a work group that is alienated from them, and they know they're going to have to go back into a losing situation. Day after day as they pull into the parking lot, the knot in their stomach tightens. What the managers of such employees are doing, supposedly out of a sense of compassion, is perpetuating a losing situation for these workers. In the name of compassion, the managers are inflicting emotional trauma and continued stress, the negative effects of which are certainly felt by the spouses and children of these workers. I submit to you that it is the most inhumane approach possible to let employees in this position suffer such prolonged emotional stress.

Turnover studies show that people who leave the organization voluntarily are generally those who have high levels of confidence, positive self-esteem, and a real belief in their own capabilities. The low-talent, low-confidence people are the ones who tend not to go out the door of their own volition. They are insecure and will hang on in bad situations because they don't believe they can do better somewhere else. They need assistance in getting to the decision point that sends them through the door into the next phase of their life.

When high-talent people encounter a difficult situation or a boss whose personality doesn't mesh well with theirs, they quickly conclude that they'll take their talents someplace else. "Who needs this chicken outfit?" is their motto. And because they have capability, and they have confidence, they walk out the door. Indeed, a real test of any organization is its effectiveness at retaining good people, because good people won't stay in poor working environments. Unfortunately, those at the other end of the scale will. People who have come to a dead end in life often find that leaving to seek a better life adjustment is something they cannot bring themselves to do on their own.

"Go Ahead. Make My Day."

When people are exit-interviewed on the day of their termination and asked, "How did you like this experience?" they report they didn't care for it a whole lot! Nobody who is terminated is overjoyed. Yet in one survey of such people a year *after* termination, about 80 percent reported that the termination was "the best thing that ever happened to me."[1] As unbelievable as it may sound, these people are now better, and better off, for the experience. Why is that?

At the point of termination, people's whole lives are turned upside down. They have to start thinking about finding a job and what it is they want in life. They start looking at want ads and going on interviews, and they come home at night and talk over each potential job, getting advice from family and friends. What tends to happen is that these people move from a point of maladjustment in their lives, where their job was not the right one, to a point where they now have a different kind of job, doing something they always wanted to do but were afraid to try. And a year later, what is found is that the terminated workers have adjusted, and the overwhelming majority of them will be feeling a lot better about self and life.

Sherman's law is not so astonishing after all: *Fire people so that they can be successful someplace else.* Termination is a great gift that you give to problem employees, a gift they needed because they lacked the understanding or motivation to actively seek a more suitable position on their own. You're going to do them a great deal of good. So termination can simply be an opportunity to help troubled workers, while at the same time solving a whole range of company problems spawned by the situation. By helping them move on to a more successful adjustment, you are taking them out of a position in which they feel enslaved and placing them in an arena where they can make choices about their lives.

None of us can guarantee the happiness or the success of any other human being. We can't do it for our own children, we can't do it for ourselves, we certainly can't do it for anyone who works for us. What we can do is help problem employees through a difficult decision point. Free them up so that they can perhaps be successful someplace else. The professional manager takes the following attitude toward the individual who is about to be fired:

> As a management professional, I'd like to succeed in getting everybody's perform-ance up to high levels. But I respect you enough that when I realize I can no longer help you or I cannot do in your life what some other manager might be able to do, then I'm not going to hold you back. I'm not going to perpetuate an unhappy exis-tence for you in a failing situation. I'm going to help you make that decision to move forward in your own life, and I'll wish you well as you go out the door.

The Termination Procedure

This section provides an overview of the seven points that constitute the actual proce-dure moving a person through a termination. This will provide you with a framework and a feel for how to deal with the process. Most managers report feeling far more comfortable with the act if it is structured and spelled out.

1. Do It Yourself, Do It Now, and Don't Pass the Buck

The task of terminating a problem employee cannot be delegated; it cannot be turned over to an assistant. There are all kinds of horror stories in American industry about managers who could not face the situation. For them, I recall W. C. Fields' famous line: "It is time to grab the bull by the tail and squarely face the situation."

Henry Ford I often could not face the situation, so he would let his problem employees report to their office for work only to find their papers and belongings gone! They had to ask, "Where's my stuff?" This indirect way of telling people the facts of life is dehumanizing and demeaning. Henry's firings were legendary. On one occasion, the terminated manager came in to work only to find the door to his office bricked up! On another occasion, a manager who seemed unable to grasp less subtle messages found himself moved into the office directly beneath Henry's own. A hole was chopped in Henry's floor, thereby creating a hole in the ceiling of the man's office on the floor below, and through that hole all day, Henry Ford I would toss his wastepaper, literally using the manager's office as a wastebasket. Don't beat around the bush with people. Give them the message, and give it to them straight.

2. Know Your Organization's Policy Constraints and Internal Procedures

Every organization is a little different. Each has some policy requirements and personnel procedures, and these have generally been pretty well thought out. They represent your firm's legal interpretation and perhaps spell out some of the simple mechanical and procedural details that will help this process move more smoothly.

In some cases, I'll hear a manager complain, "The personnel department won't let me fire this person." Of course, that is usually not the case. Most personnel executives will not only let you fire somebody, they'll go out of their way to help you do it! But if a manager goes to the personnel department without having documented his case, and without having followed procedures, and/or the manager is acting in violation of the law or policy, then the personnel department cannot support a decision to terminate, at least not at that time. The point of knowing about constraints and procedures is that they are there to protect the manager as he proceeds to remove this person from the organization. They are also there to protect the organization and its interests. And finally, and no less important, they are there to protect the employee. So all that is expected is that the proceedings will be conducted with a sense of due process and fairness and that the action taken will be subject to review. Doing things *by the book* at this point is going to prevent a lot of difficulties and problems later on.

3. Do This Task in Person

This is a task that has to be done face-to-face. It can't be handled over the phone or by memo. It should be done in as short and sweet a way as you can make it. Get to the point; do not waste a lot of time with small talk. The person probably already knows what's happening or may have a keen suspicion. So stick to the topic and don't prolong the agony. My recommendation is to view this as no more than a 15-minute conversation. There is simply no value in dragging it out into an hour-long termination session.

4. Preserve the Dignity of the Other Human Being

We do not have to prove that problem employees are terrible people in order to fire them. We do not have to run by them all the petty little things they have done or recite all the shortcomings in their character or performance. This is a time when we ought to be displaying a great deal of tact and smoothness and skill in interpersonal relations. *This session is simply an announcement of a decision.* It is not a discussion.

Under no circumstances should you discuss all the reasons why this person is being terminated; do not marshall all of your proofs or display your evidence. That advice has value primarily because you are not trying to humiliate this person, nor are you trying to send this person out the door with sour words echoing in his ears. A second reason for not turning it into a discussion is that if, in a worst-case scenario, this termination should result in legal action, the last thing in the world you want to do is show your opponent all your positions. So if you avoid getting into a discussion and avoid showing your evidence, your attorney will have a far better chance of conducting an effective defense.

One of the best executives I ever knew when it came to the actual performance of this task was someone who was so good at firing people that he was able to preserve their sense of dignity. He simply avoided assigning any blame or pointing the finger in this announcement session. As a result, people would leave the session feeling good about themselves, and even feeling good about the person who had fired them. Often the conversation went something like this:

> Tom, I think you know why we're here today. In our previous sessions and conferences together, we have both talked about how things aren't working out the way we would have liked. I know that the results you wanted haven't been there. But I also know that you've really put a lot of effort into this thing. You've taken your very best shot at it, and I have a great deal of respect for you.
>
> Therefore, this hasn't been an easy decision to make, but I've decided we must call an end to the employment relationship. It seems to me, Tom, that there are times when we have square pegs in round holes. It has always been my feeling that square pegs are fine and round holes are fine, but they just don't fit together. And I want you to know that I have no negative feelings toward you — quite the contrary, in fact.
>
> I'm sure that you're going to do well in your future assignments and that you're going to be successful. I realize that this will be a difficult time for you, and my feelings certainly go out to you and your family. But I also know that you're a big enough person to handle this problem. In the long run, Tom, I've just come to believe that it's the right thing for both of us. I want to wish you the very, very best. I have every confidence in you and in your ability to bounce back and do well again.

To some, that may sound a little hokey, but because the executive who used that approach was genuine in his relationships, the effect was positive. The words chosen are less important than the sincerity and attitude behind them. The key in this conversation is to reaffirm the departing employee's personal worth. By voicing confidence about his future and sending positive signals, it helps prevent the conversation from turning into a downer. A critical point to remember is the supersensitivity of this moment. To show any tension or, even worse, to approach the person with a belligerent attitude, is only going to evoke negative reactions. While you don't want to tell this person that he is wonderful in areas in which the person failed to perform, nothing prevents you from appreciating his value as a human being.

5. Streamline the Separation Process

I've dealt personally with over 200 terminations, and it strikes me that the smoother you can make this process, the better. I really dislike moving the terminated person from place to place in the organization after the ax has already fallen. It always seems to be a lot smoother when the discussion can be handled entirely in the manager's office. If the personnel executive normally conducts an additional separation interview, perhaps that could be done in the manager's office, as well. Do whatever is possible in this closing period to reduce the discomfort for the person being separated. If you parade the terminated worker from office to office, and make him overly visible to co-workers during a time of such pain, you will surely get an angry reaction.

If separation checks are normally given on that last day, have them already made out, and bring any other materials needed to explain what's going to happen with respect to benefit plans. Collection of keys, manuals, or any other company property should all have been thought out in advance. In some cases, the manager might accompany the employee back to his office or locker room to assist with gathering the employee's belongings and taking them out of the building.

I don't think it's wise to tell the employee that he is to work until the end of the shift or the end of the week. To leave the office after being terminated and then have to stay in the work unit for another half-day or longer doesn't make much sense. It also creates a risk of a disgruntled employee's spreading discontent among other workers. So as soon as possible after the separation discussion, get the person physically out of the building. (In some cases, the person will want time to complete a specific task, cancel appointments, or notify certain co-workers that he is leaving. If the request seems reasonable, use your judgment as to whether it should be granted.)

You should also try to be as creative and supportive about outplacement services as you can. For example, most companies have a termination policy that indicates that a couple of years of service entitle a terminated employee to only a couple of weeks of termination pay. But with a little creativity, you may be able to implement that policy more effectively. Some organizations will give the separating employee several choices, such as:

> Tom, we can handle this either as a termination or as a voluntary resignation. If we handle it as a termination, I will have to follow the policy manual and give you two weeks of separation pay. Or if, at your choice, we treat this as a voluntary resignation, I'm empowered to continue your pay for longer than two weeks — in this particular instance, for six weeks. While you physically would not be at the company, and we would collect your keys and other company property today, your actual termination date would not be until six weeks from now. This will enable you to tell prospective employers that you're still on our payroll, which should be a help to you.

(Or, as an alternative, the employer could increase the separation check to six weeks' worth of pay and issue the check to Tom that day if he elects to resign.)

> So, Tom, we can handle this on a resignation basis if you prefer to go that route, or we can handle it as a regular termination. It's your choice.

In the event that the employee chooses to resign, have prepared beforehand a brief resignation statement for him to sign. This will preclude any further legal claim of wrongful firing — you have a statement of resignation on record.

Several benefits result from providing good outplacement support. One is that the employee who is savvy about the job-hunting process will be aware that he will look better if this is handled as a resignation rather than a termination. If you have also cushioned the financial impact, you signal management's intention to make the employee's departure as comfortable and humane as possible.

Some managers get concerned about paying extra money to somebody who perhaps doesn't deserve it. I think the way to look at it is that it's cheap insurance, guaranteeing that you have done the very human thing of trying to help the person as he makes some difficult adjustments. And from a very practical standpoint, if the route of voluntary resignation is taken, the employee has in essence compromised almost completely any future claim he might care to make against the company. Some companies will go even further, paying for job-hunting costs, résumé-writing services, and the like. I am generally in favor of anything that helps the person without compromising the company's legal position.

6. Watch What Is Said to Other People

The normal reaction of other employees will be to wonder what's happened. They will naturally be curious and no doubt will have heard some of the facts and rumors surrounding the case. The hard bottom line is that it's none of their business. Just because other employees knew the terminated individual doesn't give them any right to confidential information about the case.

Amateurs in management may feel the need to justify their decision and sometimes get into arguments or discussions with the remaining employees regarding the appropriateness of that decision. Occasionally, other employees will challenge the action and voice their disapproval of it, thus prompting this defensive response. However, management is not a popularity contest, and I don't think good management is served by attempting to justify to others decisions that are made in this arena. A simple announcement that "Tom has decided to pursue other avenues in life," possibly even coupled with an expression of confidence that Tom is going to do well elsewhere, are sufficient. I don't think anything useful is served by discussing the matter further with the remaining employees.

There could be a concern on the part of other employees that Tom's departure may simply be a precursor of their own. If there are no plans to take further termination action within the unit, then it would not be amiss to put some word out that this is not

part of a wholesale reduction in force, but simply an individual decision that Tom has made, or that you have made about Tom. So calm the fears that people may have, but don't discuss the case.

Remembering to watch what is said to other employees also applies to how you handle reference checks that will later be made on the former employee. In some organizations, all reference checks are handled by the personnel department — which is the best practice. Where you don't have that staff service available, the basic rule is, "If you can't say anything nice, don't say anything at all." The safest course of action is to confirm dates of employment, job title, and whether the person is eligible for rehire. Because terminations always carry the risk of some future legal action, I wouldn't say anything else unless it is complimentary to the person. Remember, you don't know who is calling, which is why some companies require a written request before providing a reference. Of course, if the employee has elected to resign, that gives you a greater opportunity to pass along the good things that ought to be communicated. At the very least, reveal nothing regarding the basis for your displeasure with the former employee.

7. Analyze What Went Wrong

That night, as the manager goes home, a great burden will have been lifted, but it will be a sober moment. An important arena of life called employment has not worked out for someone — someone that the manager had responsibility for. Such a situation certainly calls for the manager to understand exactly what went wrong so that he or she can learn from this experience. Were selection processes defective? Did the employee get off track because of inadequate training? Did the organization fail to provide good supervisory role models for the employee to identify with? What can be learned from this? What should be done differently next time?

Summary

Those who have used the seven-step approach to termination have had good success. When you come to appreciate the underlying dynamics of why managers naturally shrink from termination, and when you begin to see that it is important to free people up, and that sometimes the best thing you can do for a problem employee is to stop doing what clearly isn't working for that person, then it is possible to succeed with this process. As managers begin to realize that termination can be handled in a humane and face-saving way, they reach a point of maturity that allows them not to dread it. While you will never welcome this task, at least you can feel confident that your decision is right and that you are handling the process properly.

You can manage employee problems and problem employees. The best way to manage them is through a step-by-step, systematic approach. The approach described in this book has a proven track record and should be effective, at least to some degree, with about half to three-quarters of the people that you're now contending with. And those with whom you can't win can be given the opportunity to win with some other manager, someplace else. In the end, you will have done everything possible. Your conscience will be clean, and you will have passed the test of being tough enough to deal with one of management's most difficult tasks.

13

Keep It Legal

In disciplining or terminating a problem employee, managers inevitably want to understand the legal constraints that will govern the decisions they want to make. We live in an increasingly litigious society where, instead of negotiating, we sue. And the courts have increasingly been handing down rulings that overturn long-standing traditions. Certainly, this has been so in a whole range of cases that affect management of the problem employee, and these have served to redefine traditional ways of looking at the workplace contract.

Earlier chapters have mentioned legal issues associated with performance appraisal systems, disciplinary procedures, and termination. This chapter will briefly review some basic principles of U.S. federal employment law, as well as patterns and trends reflected in recent court decisions. It will also suggest ways for employers to reduce their legal risks when dealing with problem employees.

The following discussion is meant only as a general guide; *a qualified attorney should be consulted for further information.*

I urge employers to get expert legal advice for several reasons. First, providing such advice is beyond the scope of this book. Second, while federal law applies anywhere in the United States and its territories, a patchwork quilt of state and local laws also apply. State and local statutes would not contradict or take precedence over national law, but in many cases, they extend beyond federal law or cover additional situations. There are also regulations that apply to certain industries, military contractors, and so on. Finally, the law is continually being refined, either by legislatures or by the courts. For all these reasons, counsel is necessary to assure that the rights of the manager and the organization, as well as those of the employee, are protected.

Employment at Will

Notwithstanding the specific statutes that may apply to a particular case, the general principles covering the handling of all problem employee situations stem from a very old concept in the law known as "employment at will." By employment at will is meant that since employees offer their services in return for compensation, they are employed at the will of the employer. That means that the employer can initiate a discipline or discharge action against an employee *for any reason — good, bad, or indifferent — as long as it is not a specifically excluded reason.*

While that is the general meaning of the concept of employment at will, there are two major exceptions to the rule. The first is that employees who are covered by an existing contract, whether a union contract or an individual employment contract, will have to be disciplined or discharged in accordance with any relevant conditions specified in that contract.

The second exclusion to the general rule of the employer's being free to redefine the employment relationship is that the discipline or discharge cannot be imposed for a reason that has previously been prohibited by law. Prohibited reasons as spelled out in federal law are not difficult for employers to comply with, since they are basically irrelevant to job performance. The factors that cannot be used to justify disciplining or discharging workers are:

Age
Sex
Race
Color
National origin
Marital status
Sexual preference
Religion or creed
Union activity or political belief

The employment at will doctrine does not allow an employer to base a discipline or discharge action on any of these characteristics. Most of these prohibitions have been enacted into law within the last 25 years and represent a major limitation on the old doctrine of employment at will.

Managers who are trying to deal with a problem employee are often overly intimidated by the applicable legal constraints. The fact is that the courts have not rejected the concept of employment at will, but have only stated that there must be fair limits on it. So the name of the game is to understand the limits as they apply and then play the game with gusto. The courts will uphold an employer's right to discipline or discharge *if* the rules have been followed. Rather than feeling that they can't take action, managers simply need to understand how to skillfully use their power to employ at will.

Due Process Restrictions

There are some additional areas beyond the protected categories of age, race, and so on where employment at will is restricted. The courts have ruled that an employer may not

discipline or discharge any employee who is involved in a due process action. For example, an employee who may have filed a complaint with a state or federal regulatory agency having jurisdiction over wages and hours must be allowed to pursue that question with the agency until a determination has been made. Depending on what the determination is, an employer may then be able to discipline or discharge the employee.

In like fashion, an employee who complains to a regulatory agency having jurisdiction over safety in the workplace, the Equal Employment Opportunity Commission or its corresponding state agency, or the National Labor Relations Board is in essence raising questions about fairness or appropriateness of treatment at work. Until these regulatory agencies have made their determination, an employer is prohibited from interfering, even though the employee may not have just cause. Even though the worker's complaint to the agency may simply be a delaying or annoying tactic, it still places him under the protection of due process.

The concept of due process is implicit in both common law and the U.S. Constitution. The courts in upholding it are basically saying to any employer, "Give the employee an opportunity to raise his question." From the court's point of view, it doesn't yet know whether the employee is right or wrong. And so the fairest thing is to go through the steps of the review process: hearing the complaint, conducting an investigation, taking time to consider the evidence, and then making a determination. This stepwise procedure involved in handling a complaint through the appropriate regulatory agency is a quasi-judicial approach that the courts look upon favorably.

Key point: Since the courts are favorably disposed toward the regulatory agencies' stepwise process of gathering information and evaluating evidence, it logically follows that when an employer provides for due process in its own grievance procedures and in its own employee handling, this will be viewed favorably by the courts. So a strategy that has to be pursued by any corporation trying to remove problem employees is to let them follow the due process road. When those approaches have finally been exhausted, it can then remove the employee, assuming there is sufficient cause.

Unjust Firings

Employment at will in recent years has had further limitations placed upon it through the enactment of new laws by state legislatures or as a result of rulings on specific cases handed down by state or federal courts. In some instances, these limitations are not yet fully defined and as such represent only an emerging pattern. Your own legal counsel can tell you whether your organization is affected by these limitations. Please keep in mind that what I'm now going to discuss applies only to certain states or certain jurisdictions or certain industries. Nonetheless, as we consider these examples, you will see the kind of thinking that is going on as the employment at will doctrine is being eroded. These examples go beyond the prohibited reasons that may not be used to justify disciplining or firing employees, and beyond the concept of not retaliating against those involved in due process. In these cases, courts have held that terminating employees under certain other circumstances will not be allowed: They will be deemed "unjust" firings.

Specific examples of this include what has been referred to as "wrongful discharge." In one case, an employee was pressured by his employer to perjure himself in a legal proceeding involving the company. The employee refused to perjure himself and lie for the firm on the stand and was later terminated by his employer. The court called that a wrongful discharge.

A second example of unjust firing was a discharge characterized by the court as involving "slander." After a firing, a prospective new employer asked the original employer to provide a letter of reference for the terminated employee. The letter contained certain negative statements that the original employer was unable to prove in court. The court held that the original employer's action was unjust.

A third example was what one court ruled the "intentional infliction of emotional abuse." In this particular case, the employee was badgered into resigning. The work environment was made extremely unpleasant, and the person was not treated with any sense of dignity or respect. In this instance, the court ruled that an employer's right to discharge does not give it the right to emotionally abuse the person.

In another case, the wording of an employment policy was held to be the basis for an unjust firing. The employee manual stated that when an employee finished the "probationary period," he would then become a "permanent employee." A so-called permanent employee was later fired and presented the case to the court. The court indicated that if a firm is going to call the person a permanent employee, that doesn't mean he suddenly loses that permanent status merely because the employer wants to initiate termination proceedings.

A similar instance involved a statement in the employee handbook that an employee finishing the probationary period would be "off probation." The "off probation" phrase was used as an argument to the court that the employee had proved to the employer his right to the job. In another case in the same vein, the employee handbook indicated that no employee would be terminated without "just cause." That promise left the employer in the position of having to prove exactly what constituted just cause, and the justness of the cause became a point of contention in court.

The courts have also ruled that it's an unjust firing if an implied contract exists. Earlier I stated that employees who are under a union contract or an individual employment contract will find that that governs their relationship with the employer. This limitation on employment at will was extended by one court in which the jurist ruled that there is such a thing as an implied contract and that statements from the supervisor or statements in the employee manual can be considered as binding as though there had been a written contract. The court ruled that it was an implied contract when a supervisor said, "Hey, when you're off probation, you've got a job here for life."

In perhaps one of the most chilling and questionable decisions handed down by a jurist, a firing was held to be unjust if the reason for the firing was "unfair or unreasonable." When it comes to what is unfair and unreasonable, I think you can readily see that such conditions are often largely in the eye of the beholder — which throws a real wild card into the employment environment. While the wording of the decision may have been somewhat unfortunate, the court was again reminding the employer that it likes things done in a neat and orderly fashion. The court favors operations characterized by due process, as well as reason and fairness in the exercise of employment at will. The courts look unfavorably on employers that seem to have acted arbitrarily, exhibiting the Wild West spirit of the old employment at will doctrine. While the ruling that an unjust firing was one that was "unfair or unreasonable" is perhaps subject to differing interpretations, it nonetheless illustrates what a court may hold to be improper.

A more clear-cut case of unjust firing was when an employer acted "against the public interest." In this particular instance, the employer was acting in an irresponsible way in terms of jeopardizing public safety, and a whistle-blower, an employee on the payroll, brought it to the attention of the local press. The court held that whistle-blowers had to be protected. In practice, however, whistle-blowers are pretty much dead in the organization politically thereafter, even if they are able to preserve their jobs. Nonetheless, the courts have held that the public interest will prevail in such cases and will be considered more important than the employer's right to maintain the employment at will doctrine.

Another finding of unjust firing was for "fraudulently induced employment." This can occur when an employee had joined the organization or accepted a transfer within it based on unkept promises. Such promises may involve the offer of monies or promotions, a favorable settlement, a specific assignment, or some other inducement that is later not delivered. The employee is frustrated, performs badly, and is fired. When the employer breaks promises, the court may consider the employment at will doctrine to have been set aside.

One final example of this increasingly difficult thicket of legal rulings is that it's been held to be unjust for the employer to "deal negligently" with the employee. It has been considered management negligence not to tell an employee specifically what he is expected to do, and if the employee says to a judge, "If I had been told what it was that they wanted me to do better, I would have done it better," the court may rule negligence on the part of management as the reason why this employee has not performed up to expectations. If the employer can show no evidence that a reasonable effort has been made to teach the employee how to perform the work acceptably, the case may be unwinnable. While this is almost a catch-22 situation, it does say that for the employment at will doctrine to prevail, the employer must in fact have expended some demonstrable effort to turn the person around before exercising its authority to fire, except in cases calling for summary discharge.

The Bottom Line

Having said all that, and perhaps having scared you half to death in doing so, let me emphatically draw this conclusion: If you have someone who deserves termination or who needs to be disciplined in some other fashion, do not be intimidated by these legal constraints. Your first responsibility is to the corporation, to whatever action is appropriate in your particular situation, and it's on that basis that you must make your decisions. Never be afraid and never refrain from taking the corrective action that must be taken. And for heaven's sake, don't let the attorneys run your business! So don't back away from the problem, and don't let your freedom of action be hampered by fears of lawsuits.

I guess what I'm saying is, move ahead, but move ahead deliberately, in a stepwise fashion, following your procedure and policy manuals, in line with applicable state statutes and federal law, and never overstepping the areas that are specifically prohibited or that violate due process.

Practical Pointers to Prevent Legal Troubles

Several other tactics that managements might employ in order to avoid being hoisted by their own petard would be to remove from correspondence and manuals any language that implies a promise of continued employment. The concept that everyone is always, in a sense, on probation should be expressed both in correspondence and in personnel policies.

A second suggestion, in order to keep your options open, is that the first three months, six months, twelve months, or whatever your normal probationary period now is, should no longer be referred to as a probationary period, but rather an "introductory period" or a "beginning period" with the employer. This gets rid of the question of, "Am I, or am I not, on probation?"

A third specific recommendation is to deal consistently with all employees so that variations in practice can't be misconstrued. A common problem in organizations is that policies will be interpreted differently from one manager to another. When interpretations vary so widely, you no longer have any policy. The courts may rule that the actual practice is policy, even if that practice is totally different from what appears in the policy manual. Let me restate that: Practice will be considered to take precedence over policy. So deal consistently with people. One of the best ways to do that is to make sure that all termination or disciplinary procedures are coordinated by the corporate personnel department so that there will be some control over this process. That means that corporate personnel people may turn down some managers who want to fire when those managers are not in conformance with the practice that has been followed in other parts of the organization.

One technique that is used by some companies is to have employees sign a statement at the time of employment to the effect that their jobs are "at will" and are continued at the employer's option. In order to cover existing employees who had not been presented with such a statement at the time of employment, one company had the statement signed by employees at the time they received their next salary increase. It seems to me that the latter practice particularly may make your organization look a little paranoid in the eyes of your employees. It's a question of how far you want to go in this area.

Some firms, for example, will put no discharges in writing, not wanting to provide any documents to the departing employee at the time of termination. At one level, these kinds of administrative measures can protect you. At another level, they can make you look a little foolish. Because the handling of these matters becomes a real judgment call, your approach should be discussed carefully beforehand, and some company policy should be established to help you deal with them.

Beyond these administrative concerns, you may want to go back and reread the chapters in this book that describe the positive prevention of problem employees and the positive discipline practices that should apply once trouble begins to surface. The recommendations presented there represent a step-by-step due process approach. The documentation, feedback mechanisms, and assessment procedures that will form the basis of an excellent legal case are already incorporated into these approaches. That is, one of the best ways to deal with the legal aspects of a particular situation is to have followed the preventive measures and the positive-discipline steps that are outlined in this book.

Some Key Legal Questions to Make Sure You're Right

There are certain key questions that always arise in considering the legal issues surrounding problem employee management, discipline, and termination. Did the employer deal *fairly* with the employee? To deal fairly obviously means that there has been no discrimination against people in the "protected" categories. Has the company treated a female employee differently than a male employee? Has it treated a younger employee differently than an older worker? Dealing fairly also means that there's been some honest effort to help the person overcome his difficulty.

A second key question to ask to make sure you're on safe ground: Have the processes been *objective*? Have ratings been given, feedback provided? Have there been training programs? Have disciplinary warnings been put in writing? Is there some evidence to support the claim of poor performance? Where the employer has been as objective as it's possible to be under sometimes emotional circumstances, that looks good and is viewed favorably by the courts.

A third major legal concern is whether there is evidence of *consistency*. Is there any reason to believe that the employer has treated this particular case differently than it has treated other similar cases? For instance, have other chronic latecomers been retained while this particular employee has been fired? Have certain classes of jobs or certain departments been given preferential treatment?

Summary

The increasingly litigious nature of today's society has made many managers extremely wary about dealing firmly with problem employees — even in cases where such action is clearly warranted. These concerns are to some extent justified. However, a sound understanding of the laws and principles governing employee management, discipline, and termination, together with the assistance of competent legal counsel and a commitment on the part of the employer to fairness and consistency in the treatment of employees, will put the employer on solid legal ground.

A number of major legal considerations affect employment issues. The first is employment at will (the concept that the employer can take any discipline or discharge action that isn't specifically prohibited by law). Two major exceptions to the employment at will doctrine are that employees covered by an existing contract are protected by provisions of that contract and that employers cannot discipline or discharge an employee for such prohibited reasons as the worker's age, race, religion, and so on.

Employment at will is also subject to due process restrictions—namely, that if an employee has filed a work-related complaint with the applicable state or federal agency, the employer must refrain from taking action against the employee until the issue in question has been taken through the steps of the agency's formal review process and a finding has been handed down. As an extension of this position, the courts look favorably upon provisions for due process within a firm's own employment practices.

Employment at will is being further eroded by an emerging body of legal rulings that provide a still-evolving definition of what is meant by an "unjust firing" or a "wrongful discharge." These rulings cover a wide range of varied issues and in many cases are not uniformly applicable to all employment situations but rather are binding only on a given state or industry. The vital lesson for managers is that they must maintain an ongoing familiarity with court rulings affecting their particular employment situation, to ensure that their actions will be found justified in the event of legal action.

There are certain steps employers can take in order to protect their legal position. Among these are such measures as exercising care in the wording of correspondence with employees, eliminating discrepancies in company practice that could be construed as favoring or discriminating against certain workers, and having employees sign a statement acknowledging the employer's option to continue or discontinue their jobs "at will." Employers can also ask themselves certain key questions regarding the fairness, objectivity, and consistency of their treatment of employees as a means of identifying and correcting practices that could constitute grounds for legal action.

What it all comes down to is that where employers can show the court they have been fair, they have been objective, and they have been consistent, there is very good reason to believe they will win any case that may be brought against them. Again I say, go back and look at the positive prevention procedures previously outlined, along with those for positive discipline, because they have built into them those aspects for fairness, objectivity, and consistency that the courts are looking for. And I think that not only will you satisfy the courts, but you'll satisfy yourself. You'll know that you have done your job right. You'll have no reason to apologize or feel bad about the decisions that you've made. In the final analysis, we all have to satisfy our own internal judge and answer to the court of self-respect. Following the procedures that have been outlined in this book will allow you to do that.

Notes

Notes for Chapter 1

1. Sylvester Stallone, *Rocky II* (New York: Ballantine Books, a Division of Random House, Inc., 1979), p. 2.
2. *As You Like It,* Act II, Scene 1, *The Complete Works of Shakespeare* W. J. Craig, ed. (London: Oxford University Press, 1908), p. 241.
3. Reprinted by permission of the *Harvard Business Review.* Excerpt from "Pygmalion in Management," by Sterling Livingston, July/August 1969. Copyright © 1969 by the President and Fellows of Harvard College; all rights reserved.

Notes for Chapter 2

1. Lester R. Bittel, *What Every Supervisor Should Know* (New York: McGraw-Hill, 1985), p. 327.
2. Ibid., p. 330.

Note for Chapter 4

1. Sterling Livingston, "Pygmalion in Management," *Harvard Business Review* (July/August 1969), pp. 81–89.

Notes for Chapter 5

1. Robert M. Guion, *Personnel Testing* (New York: McGraw-Hill, 1965), p. 467.
2. Ibid., p. 475.

Notes for Chapter 9

1. The discussion in this chapter's sections on "The Emotionally Disturbed" and "Emotional First Aid" is paraphrased and summarized from Lester R. Bittel, *What Every Supervisor Should Know* (New York: McGraw-Hill, 1985), pp. 334–36, supplemented by my own commentary.
2. Ibid., p. 337.
3. Ibid., pp. 340–41. The discussion here is a paraphrase of Bittel's summary.
4. This information is based on a report of actual experience with accident repeaters that I received in 1976 while a corporate director of human resources.
5. Bittel, *What Every Supervisor Should Know*, p. 336.
6. Ibid., p. 337.

Note for Chapter 12

1. From a 1976 survey I performed while a corporate human resources executive.

Index